3

RIGHTS IN AIR SPACE

THE MELLAND SCHILL LECTURES

*delivered at the University of Manchester
and published by the University Press*

The Law of International Institutions in Europe,
by A. H. Robertson, B.C.L., S.J.D., Spring, 1961

The Role of International Law in the Elimination of War,
by Professor Quincy Wright, Winter, 1961

The Acquisition of Territory in International Law,
by Professor R. Y. Jennings, Winter, 1962

The Sources and Evidences of International Law,
by Clive Parry, LL.D., Spring, 1965

Rights in Air Space,
by D. H. N. Johnson, M.A., LL.B., October, 1965

The Foreign Office and the Practitioner,
by Sir Francis A. Vallat, K.C.M.G., Q.C., 1965 and 1966

The International Law of the Sea,
by D. W. Bowett, M.A., LL.B., Ph.D., 1966

OTHER BOOKS IN INTERNATIONAL LAW

Self-Defence in International Law,
by D. W. Bowett, M.A., LL.B., Ph.D.

Human Rights in Europe,
by A. H. Robertson, B.C.L., S.J.D.

The Legal Problems of Foreign Investment in Developing Countries,
by E. I. Nwogugu, LL.B., Ph.D.

RIGHTS
IN
AIR SPACE

by

D.H.N. JOHNSON

Professor of International and Air Law at the
London School of Economics and Political Science

MANCHESTER UNIVERSITY PRESS

U.S.A.: OCEANA PUBLICATIONS INC.

© 1965, Manchester University Press

Published by the University of Manchester at
THE UNIVERSITY PRESS
316–324 Oxford Road, Manchester, 13

U.S.A.
OCEANA PUBLICATIONS INC.
40 Cedar Street, Dobbs Ferry, N.Y.
Library of Congress Catalog Card Number 65–15974

Printed in Great Britain by Butler & Tanner Ltd, Frome and London

FOREWORD

By her Will, the late Miss Olive Schill of Prestbury, Cheshire, an old friend of the University, whose portrait is painted in Lady Katharine Chorley's 'Manchester Made Them', left the sum of £10,000 to the University in memory of her brother, Melland Schill, who died in the 1914–1918 war. The annual income from this sum is to be used to promote and publish a series of public lectures of the highest possible standard dealing with International Law.

Professor Johnson is the first Professor to hold a combined Chair of International and Air Law in the United Kingdom, and in these lectures he surveys the development of Air Law from its earliest beginnings to the latest and most important conventions on the subject. Now that we are all potential travellers by air we all have an interest in the development of the legal position with regard to this now commonplace form of locomotion. The general reader, as well as the law student, should find this clear and interesting account of a new branch of law both fascinating and informative. The work should also be of great interest to those many experts who run the ever-growing air services in the world today, and not least to students of the air arm in war.

B. A. WORTLEY

Department of International Law
Law Faculty
University of Manchester

CONTENTS

PREFACE

IN introducing this small work, which I hope will contribute to a more extended understanding of air law in time of war as well as in time of peace, I wish to make a number of acknowledgements. I should like to express my thanks to the University of Manchester for the invitation to deliver the Melland Schill lectures; to Professor Wortley for his constant encouragement during their preparation; and to the staff of the Manchester University Press for the assistance they have given in preparing the text of the lectures for publication. I am also indebted to Dr. Bin Cheng, a leading authority on air law and a colleague in the University of London, for having read the proofs and made certain suggestions; and to Mr. K. O. Parsons, a member of the staff of the British Library of Political and Economic Science, for assistance with the checking of references. Finally, I want to thank the Secretary General of the International Civil Aviation Organization for having supplied the information contained in Appendix II.

All the opinions expressed in the book are, however, entirely my own.

D. H. N. JOHNSON

Chapter I

THE DEVELOPMENT OF AVIATION

INTRODUCTION

THESE lectures belong to a series devoted to the study of international law from the point of view of territory, my particular task being to deal with that part of territory which is called 'air space'.

Writers on international law have naturally enough often drawn a distinction between the law relating to the land and the law relating to the sea. Of these the law relating to the land was regarded as basic. According to Judge Huber, in the *Island of Palmas* case (1928), 'The development of the national organization of States during the last few centuries and, as a corollary, the development of international law, *have established this principle of the exclusive competence of the State in regard to its own territory in such a way as to make it the point of departure in settling most questions that concern international relations.*'[1] By 'exclusive competence' or 'sovereignty' Judge Huber meant 'independence' or, more specifically, the right, in regard to a portion of the globe, to exercise 'to the exclusion of any other State, the functions of a State'. Judge Huber also contrasted the situation, where 'territorial sovereignty belongs always to one, or in exceptional circumstances to several States, to the exclusion of all others', with the situation where 'the functions of a State can be performed by *any* State'.[2] This latter situation, he said, is 'precisely the characteristic feature of the legal situation pertaining in those parts of the globe which, like the high seas or lands without a master, cannot or do not yet form the territory of a State'.[3]

Thus, Judge Huber drew a fundamental distinction between territory under the sovereignty of a State on the one hand, and, on the other hand, areas such as the high seas and *territorium nullius* which were not under the sovereignty of a State. According to this way of thinking, the law relating to the land derived its importance from two considerations: first, that international law was considered as a system applying between land-possessing States; and secondly, that

---

[1] *Reports of International Arbitral Awards*, Vol. 2, p. 831, at p. 838. Italics added.
[2] Ibid. Italics added.   [3] Ibid.

1

the possession of land was considered necessary to the existence of a State. The nomadic tribe, even though it might consist of people, have a government and wander over land, was often quoted as an example of a community which could not be a subject of international law, since it had not settled down on, and did not actually possess, a given area of territory. Again, no-one conceived of a fleet at sea, however powerful, as having a status under international law distinct from that of the Power which equipped it and on whose ports it was based.[1]

Notwithstanding the overriding importance of land, there are many reasons why the law relating to the sea has always been regarded by international lawyers as of the greatest significance. In the first place, there is the antiquity of this branch of the law. The Rolls of Oleron preceded by many centuries the emergence of detailed rules of international law concerning land territory. Secondly, there is the plain geographical fact that over seventy per cent of the surface of the globe is covered by sea. Thirdly, the sea has always been a major area of contact between the nations, whether in the form of friendly intercourse and trade, or of various kinds of conflict.

Poised somewhat uneasily between the law of land territory and the law of the sea proper was the law governing territorial waters. The best known example of the uncertain position of this law was the decision of the Court for Crown Cases Reserved in *The Queen* v. *Keyn*[2] in which it held that the English courts were without jurisdiction to try the master of a German ship which had been in collision with a British steamer two and a half miles off Dover. The decision was a curious amalgam of English law and international law. According to Sir Alexander Cockburn, the Lord Chief Justice, 'No proposition of law can be more incontestable or more universally admitted than that, according to the general law of nations, a foreigner, though criminally responsible to the law of a nation not his own for acts done by him while within the limits of its territory, cannot be made responsible to its law for acts done beyond such limits.' This alleged rule of international law was, however, qualified by a rule of municipal law to the effect that 'if the legislature of a particular country should think fit by express enactment to render foreigners subject to its law with reference to offences committed beyond the limits of its territory, it would be incumbent on the Courts of such country

---

[1] If the proposed NATO multilateral nuclear force (MLF) should ever come into existence, even this basic concept might be challenged.
[2] [1876] 2 Ex. D. 63.

to give effect to such enactment, leaving it to the State to settle the question of international law with the Governments of other nations'.

These remarks demonstrate with striking clarity the importance of ascertaining the 'limits of territory' in international law.

In the same case Lord Chief Justice Cockburn proceeded to hold that 'unless . . . Keyn, at the time the offence of which he has been convicted was committed, was on British territory or on board a British ship, he could not be properly brought to trial under English law, in the absence of express legislation'. Keyn, who certainly was not on board a British ship, was found also not to be on British territory either, since 'it may be asserted without fear of contradiction that the position that the sea within a belt or zone of three miles from the shore . . . forms part of the realm or territory of the Crown is a doctrine unknown to the ancient law of England'. It was admitted that there was a great deal of international authority to support the theory that each State has sovereignty over a belt of sea extending to the range of cannon from the coast. At the same time it was asserted that 'in the practical application of the rule, in respect of the particular of distance, as also in the still more essential particular of the character and degree of sovereignty and dominion to be exercised, great difference of opinion and uncertainty have prevailed, and still continue to exist'.

So far as Great Britain was concerned, this particular uncertainty was put an end to by the Territorial Waters Jurisdiction Act, 1878, which provides that 'an offence committed by a person, whether he is or is not a subject of her Majesty' is an offence within the jurisdiction of the English courts provided it was committed 'within one marine league of the coast measured from low-water mark'. That was the combined effect of Sections 2 and 7 of the Act. It was also made clear, however, in Section 7 that British territorial waters *as such* consist more vaguely of 'such part of the sea adjacent to the coast of the United Kingdom, or the coast of some other part of Her Majesty's dominions, as is deemed by international law to be within the territorial sovereignty of Her Majesty' and are not necessarily limited, except for the purposes of the exercise of criminal jurisdiction under the Act, to a belt of three miles only.

It may be asked why it has been thought necessary to refer to this ancient controversy about territorial waters in a course of lectures on air space. The reason is that this controversy was fresh in people's minds when, shortly afterwards, with the invention of the power-driven aeroplane, it became necessary with great suddenness to

3

change international law from a two-dimensional into a three-dimensional system and to take up a position on rights in air space.

The law of the sea is outside my terms of reference in these lectures, except in so far as I must refer to it incidentally owing to the considerable effect which it has had upon the development of rules for the air space. I cannot, however, fail to draw your attention to the fact that, owing to the inventions of modern science, international law is once again undergoing a major change of scale—this time, you might say, from a three-dimensional to a four-dimensional system. Having during the last sixty years assimilated, not without difficulty, the law of the air space, international law now finds itself having to accommodate as well the law of 'outer space', or simply the law of 'space', as it is sometimes called.

It is possible, and perhaps desirable, that in course of time a single law of the 'aerospace'—a handy term sometimes used to describe both 'air space' and 'outer space' together—will be developed. In international law as it stands at present, however, there is a tendency to distinguish between 'air space' and 'outer space' or simply 'space'. A separate 'Space Law' is indeed being elaborated under our very eyes. The process of its elaboration—through the actions and claims of States, by means of their protests and failures to protest; through their attitudes in deliberative bodies such as the General Assembly of the United Nations; through the resolutions of non-governmental organizations; through analogies taken from maritime law and air law; and finally, perhaps, even through the views of writers—provides a fascinating, up-to-date and practical means of checking the many theories that exist about the 'sources of international law'.[1] But this process, too, absorbing though it is, is outside the scope of these lectures.

My task then is to concentrate on the international law of the air, and mainly on that particular branch of that law which is concerned with the air space as such.

I shall not therefore attempt to deal, except incidentally, with questions of municipal law, including private international law, important though these are in the general complex of aviation law.

Exponents of air law have not been slow to assert the independence of their subject. 'Le droit aérien,' says M. Nicolas Mateesco Matte, 'est une science juridique autonome.'[2]

---

[1] See R. Y. Jennings in *International and Comparative Law Quarterly*, 13 (1964) p. 385.
[2] *Traité de droit aérien-aéronautique* (2nd ed., 1964), p. 61.

In this spirit chairs and institutes have been founded for the study of air law; many treatises have been written on it; and even journals have been started for the regular and methodical development of the new discipline. All this is to the good. It can, however, be overdone. It would be disastrous, for instance, if air lawyers thought they could develop their discipline without paying the closest attention to the links between air law and public international law. Similarly, in this day and age, aeronautical questions deserve extensive consideration in any treatise on public international law. I contend therefore that the forty-odd pages devoted to aeronautical matters in the latest available editions of Oppenheim's two-volume treatise[1] are no longer commensurate with the significance these matters now possess in international law.

I recognize that the lectures which follow suffer from many limitations. But I trust that a failure to stress the links between air law and public international law will not be one of them.

I shall devote the rest of this lecture to considering briefly the development of aviation itself, and the beginning of air law. In the next lecture I shall outline the evolution of the international law of the air in the period between the first flight of a power-driven aeroplane (1903) and the outbreak of the First World War (1914). In the third lecture I shall deal with the First World War, the Paris Convention (1919) and the Hague Air Warfare Rules (1923). In the fourth lecture I shall discuss the air warfare of the Second World War. In the fifth and final lecture I shall consider three specific problems in contemporary air law, namely (i) civil aviation under the Chicago Convention (1944); (ii) trespassing in national air space; and (iii) crimes committed on board aircraft.

For most writers on air law, it is either the commercial and economic aspects, or else the problem of the liability of airline operators, that are of predominant interest. If it turns out that I stress the military and security aspect rather more than is usually done, this will be because I feel that this side of air law has been unduly neglected. In particular, some explanation, or at least some investigation, is needed as to how it came about that, after developing over a period of three hundred years the distinction between combatants and non-combatants in warfare, and after steadily improving the protection available to non-combatants, international law suddenly went into reverse on these important matters. No doubt, in order

[1] *International Law*, Vol. 1 (8th ed., by Lauterpacht, 1955) and Vol. 2 (7th ed., by Lauterpacht, 1952), London, Longmans, Green.

to explain this regression adequately, it would be necessary to make a full comparison between modern, total, ideological war and the limited hostilities of previous eras. That would carry me far beyond the scope of these lectures, even if I were competent to undertake so ambitious a task. But in so far as the development of aviation was one of the contributory factors involved, I feel I must attempt some investigation of a phenomenon which, after all, amounts not merely to a momentous change in the nature of warfare but also to a no less significant metamorphosis in the character of international law.

As Baron Van Asbeck pointed out in his remarkable valedictory lecture a few years ago, the last century has witnessed many changes in international law. 'One can observe,' he said, 'the passage from a world of separate States, weakly linked together and weakly bound by an unstable *State-law*, towards a world in which the possibilities are being explored of establishing an order in which public authority is exercised by strong institutions under a genuine *law of nations*, which binds peoples and governments by its own force and authority.' Yet, as Baron Van Asbeck also said, 'As long as the antagonism in fundamental convictions continues to divide the world, the road to an international legal order for the world as a whole lies barred, and we have to continue to live in a political order'.[1] In other words, the strides forward which international law has made in some directions have been offset by failures in other areas where this system had previously achieved some degree of success.

The world political order, of which Baron Van Asbeck spoke, rests on a balance of terror and the threat of mutual nuclear destruction. Now the way to the nuclear counter-city strategies of today lay through the acceptance, perhaps regretful, perhaps supine, perhaps even fatalist, nevertheless the acceptance, of the massive area bombardments of the Second World War. Who can doubt that much of the malaise in international law today, much of the apathy and even contempt towards it felt by all sections of opinion, from professors of international relations down to the man in the street, is due to the belief that it has no force behind it, that it commands no respect, that it is powerless to save civilization, and is even irrelevant? These attitudes towards international law are not new, but they have been intensified of late by many developments, among which I would include the failure to subject the science of aeronautics, and now astronautics, to an adequate rule of law as one of the most important.

[1] *International and Comparative Law Quarterly*, 11 (1962) pp. 1054–72. Italics in original. See especially, pp. 1055 and 1071.

Confronted with this situation, an international lawyer must face the facts, however unpalatable. But facing the facts requires some consideration of how the facts came about. That then will be my justification for including in my study of rights (and wrongs) in air space, a brief, even if unfashionable, examination of the laws of air warfare.

THE BEGINNING OF AERONAUTICS

On 19 September 1783, the brothers Montgolfier, after experimenting with paper bags in the kitchen of their home near Lyons, succeeded, in the presence of Louis XVI and his court, in sending to a height of 1500 feet a silk balloon filled with hot air, carrying a rooster, a sheep and a duck in a small gondola. All emerged safe from the experiment, except that the rooster suffered a broken wing, probably from a kick by the sheep. Shortly afterwards the king offered a criminal for a manned flight. But, establishing a tradition which has persisted into the pioneering stages of machine-powered aviation— and even astronautics—for flight to be considered a pursuit essentially worthy of 'officers and gentlemen', M. Pilâtre de Rozier, Louis XVI's historian, and the Marquis d'Arlandes went up instead. They stayed aloft for twenty-five minutes and covered a short distance. Watching this experiment, Benjamin Franklin observed that it was 'by no means a trifling one'. He hoped wistfully that it might convince sovereigns of the folly of wars, since it would be impossible for even the most potent of them to protect their kingdoms against a sudden descent of enemy balloonists.

The next year the craze spread to Britain causing Dr. Johnson, balloon enthusiast though he seems to have been, to say, 'The vehicles can serve no use till we can guide them.'

The problem of controlling flight, however, proved more difficult than that of achieving it. Despite this problem and other setbacks, including the death of de Rozier owing to an explosion, the new science continued to make progress. In 1785 an American, John Jeffries, and a Frenchman, François Blanchard, crossed from Dover to Calais in a balloon. Naturally it was not long before aviation began to be exploited for military purposes. In the French Revolutionary Wars captive balloons were used for artillery spotting, being employed even as far afield as Egypt. The Austrians tried bomb-laden balloons at the siege of Venice in 1849, but most of these were carried away from the target. Some even drifted back and exploded over the

Austrian lines. Balloons were also used at Solferino in 1859, and again in the American Civil War; but not to much effect. A sensation was caused when Gambetta and over a hundred and fifty other persons escaped from Paris in balloons during the Franco-Prussian war. More important was the controversy caused by the claims of the Prussians in that war to be entitled to treat as spies persons passing over their lines in balloons. Commenting on this pretension, a leading English international lawyer of the period, W. E. Hall, said: 'Neither secrecy, nor disguise, nor pretence being possible to persons travelling in balloons, the view taken by the Germans is inexplicable.'[1] Hall's view commended itself generally to Governments, and Article 22 of the Declaration of Brussels (1874) provided that persons passing over the enemy's lines in a balloon were not to be considered as spies.

As early as 1836, Mr. Robert Holland, M.P., and two other gentlemen were conveyed in a balloon from London to the Duchy of Nassau, a distance of 500 miles. But it was not until 1884 that a really controlled flight was made. This was the short circular tour of Renard and Krebs in an electrically-powered 'dirigible' consisting of an envelope of Chinese silk and a car of bamboo trelliswork. In 1900 Count Ferdinand von Zeppelin put into the air the first airship to bear his famous name, and in 1903 Orville and Wilbur Wright made the first controlled flight in an aeroplane at Kitty Hawk, North Carolina. Their machine was a biplane, but the machine in which Louis Blériot became the first man to make an aeroplane flight across the English Channel in 1909 was a monoplane. In their war against Turkey in 1911 the Italians used both airships and aeroplanes. (Both these types are self-propelled and dirigible, the difference between the two being that an 'airship' is lighter than air and an 'aeroplane' heavier than air.)

During the ensuing decades aircraft continued to increase in size, strength, power, speed, range, carrying capacity, and above all numbers. All these improvements had in their way effects upon the development of air law which we must consider. But it was not until the invention of gas-turbine propulsion that there was another major technological breakthrough. This became a factor of military importance towards the end of the Second World War, while the introduction of jet commercial aircraft on a large scale from 1959 onwards caused a *bouleversement* from which the airlines are only just beginning to recover financially. Now the supersonic era is almost

[1] *International Law* (1880) p. 464.

upon us and, with space flight too becoming more common, we are perhaps on the threshold of a period of technological change which will have drastic consequences for the law.

The history of aviation abounds in romantic exploits, such as the first transatlantic flight of Alcock and Brown in 1919, followed by the first solo flight across that ocean by Lindbergh eight years later. More important from our point of view was the opening up of air routes on a commercial, if not always profitable, basis. Even before the First World War zeppelins operated scheduled services between Friedrichshafen and Dusseldorf. The great increase in engine power achieved during that war, as well as the large number of surplus machines available at the end of the conflict, rendered possible the introduction of commercial aeroplane services on an extensive scale. Despite her defeat, Germany seems to have been first in the field, with a service between Berlin and Weimar, opened on 5 February 1919. During the next few months regular services began between Paris and London, between Paris and Brussels and between London and Brussels. The well-known name of KLM appeared on the scene in 1920 with a service between Amsterdam and London. Imperial Airways was formed in 1924, and by this time symptoms which have plagued European aviation ever since, excess capacity and reliance on subsidies, were already painfully apparent.

In the United States, although a few minor services were operated before the First World War, commercial aviation got off to a relatively slow start. The distances there were almost too great to make air transport feasible with the equipment then available. In 1918, however, a great step forward was taken when the Post Office, using converted Army aircraft, began an air mail route between New York and Washington, the service being extended as far as San Francisco two years later. By 1927 Pan American Airways was operating between Florida and Cuba, and two years later between Florida and Chile. In 1935 PAA began a transpacific service between San Francisco and Manila, and in the same year Imperial Airways extended to Australia the route it had for some time been operating as far as Karachi. In 1936 the famous zeppelin 'Hindenburg' began a regular service across the North Atlantic, but a year later it was destroyed by fire. Just before the Second World War began, PAA had started to operate flying-boat services from Long Island to Lisbon and Southampton. Naturally, the conflict led to a disruption of civil air services, but transatlantic flights became common and much experience was gained. When hostilities ended, the stage was set for a massive and sustained expansion of civil aviation.

THE BEGINNING OF AIR LAW

It is generally agreed that the first piece of legislation connected with aviation was the regulation made by the Paris police in 1784 prohibiting balloon flights without special permits. Other European cities followed with similar enactments. But the question of an international air law does not seem to have become a live one until the end of the nineteenth century.

What made it so in the first instance were the military rather than the civil potentialities of aviation. I have already referred to the provision in the Declaration of Brussels (1874) that a person was not to be considered as a spy merely because he passed over the enemy's lines in a balloon. At the First Hague Peace Conference (1899) a Declaration was signed in which the Contracting Powers agreed 'to prohibit, for a term of five years, the discharge of projectiles and explosives from balloons or by other new methods of a similar nature'. It is reasonable to assume that these 'other new methods' included methods depending upon the science of aeronautics, although a power-driven aeroplane had not yet flown. However, the Declaration was only to be binding upon the Contracting Powers in case of war between two or more of them, and even then not when one of the belligerents was joined by a non-Contracting Power. In the Declaration, which was ratified by twenty-four States (not including Great Britain)—whereas the Brussels Declaration was never ratified —reference was made to the Declaration of St. Petersburg of 1868. In this instrument the Contracting Parties, after referring to the work of an International Military Commission, which had 'fixed the technical limits at which the necessities of war ought to yield to the requirements of humanity', had declared as follows:

Considering that the progress of civilization should have the effect of alleviating as much as possible the calamities of war:

That the only legitimate object which States should endeavour to accomplish during war is to weaken the military force of the enemy;

That for this purpose it is sufficient to disable the greatest possible number of men;

That this object would be exceeded by the employment of arms which uselessly aggravate the sufferings of disabled men, or render their death inevitable;

That the employment of such arms would, therefore, be contrary to the laws of humanity;

The Contracting Parties engage, mutually, to renounce, in case of war among themselves, the employment, by their military or naval forces, of any projectile of less weight than four hundred grammes, which is explosive, or is charged with fulminating or inflammable substances.

The occasion of the St. Petersburg Declaration was that the Russians had developed a bullet to be used for blowing up ammunition wagons. The bullet exploded on contact with even a soft substance. The philosophy underlying the Declaration was that such explosive bullets should be banned because their use would cause unnecessary suffering to individual persons whom they might hit. The Declaration, however, was drafted in such a way that the use of explosive shells, designed to kill large numbers of men, remained legal.

Also, notwithstanding the humanitarian sentiments expressed in the preamble to the St. Petersburg Declaration, it would be erroneous to conclude that the use of any weapon which then or thereafter should offend against those sentiments would be illegal. The Declaration could not do more than it purported to do, which was simply to ban the employment of bullets that were *both* of small weight *and* 'explosive or charged with fulminating or inflammable substances'. So far as new weapons are concerned, their use, in the absence of treaty provisions, is governed by the following two principles of customary international law, viz.:

(i) A weapon is not necessarily illegal just because it is new;
(ii) The fact that it is not possible to exploit a new weapon (be it a submarine, a form of bomb, or anything else) to the full without violating an existing rule of law is not a sufficient excuse for violating that rule of law.

The situation created by the second of these two principles, however, imposes a great strain on the law. It is best resolved by a specific agreement banning the use of the new weapons or, if that is not possible, by some adjustment in the rules of war rendering legitimate at any rate a restrained use of the new weapon. If agreement along either of these lines is not achieved, the tension is likely to be resolved in war by the weapon being used by both sides and, if existing rules are violated in the process, by such use being justified as a reprisal for alleged breaches of the laws of war by the other side.

At The Hague in 1899 it was felt that the use of balloons for the purpose of discharging projectiles was attended by too many uncertainties to be permitted. But the prospect that greater accuracy might soon be obtained was also the reason for limiting the Declaration to five years.

It would be wrong to imagine that the sole preoccupation of those interested in air law at this stage was with military questions. The fifteen years that elapsed between 1899 and the outbreak of the First World War in 1914 were indeed the great creative period of air law, and the only real parallels we have to it are the enormous literary output that there was in regard to the continental shelf just after the Second World War and that there has been in regard to space law during the last decade. Among the pioneers of air law, the name of Paul Fauchille will always be remembered. This great French lawyer, as the *rapporteur* for the Institute of International Law on the subject entitled 'Régime juridique des aérostats'[1] submitted to the Brussels meeting of the Institute in 1902 a draft code containing thirty-two articles. The first seven articles were given over to general provisions; Articles 8 to 20 prescribed a regime for peacetime; and the remaining articles concerned the laws of war.

What interests us most today about Fauchille's code is some of the first articles in the draft. Article 1, for instance, drew a basic distinction between public and private aircraft, the former category being further divided into 'military' and 'civil'. Article 2 required all aircraft to carry the national colours in some convenient form. Article 3 forbade aircraft to wear colours other than those of the nation to which they belonged. So far as private machines were concerned, aircraft would belong to a country by virtue of being entered on a register kept by that country, and in order to qualify for admission to the register the owner, commander and three-quarters of the crew of the aircraft must be nationals of the country concerned.

Only when he reached Article 7 did Fauchille broach the question of air space. Here he prescribed as follows:

L'air est libre. Les Etats n'ont sur lui en temps de paix et en temps de guerre que les droits nécessaires à leur conservation. Ces droits sont relatifs à la repression de l'espionnage, à la police douanière, à la police sanitaire et aux nécessités de la défense.

Fauchille justified by somewhat theoretical reasons his doctrine of the freedom of the air. These were, firstly, that air, because of its very nature, was not capable of appropriation at all; and secondly, that

[1] The word actually used by Fauchille was 'aérostats'. Technically an 'aérostat' is a lighter-than-air craft, such as a balloon or airship. But it is reasonable to suppose that Fauchille would have applied the same principles to all types of aircraft.

since a State could not occupy air, it could not be sovereign over it. Similar theories had for centuries been put forward in support of the doctrine of the freedom of the seas, although in fact that doctrine had come to be accepted for the essentially practical reason that it best suited the changing interests of the major maritime powers.

Fauchille was sufficient of a realist to comprehend that the States for whose benefit he was preparing a code would never accept the freedom of the air in the extreme form that his theories, pushed to their logical conclusion, might demand. Even the freedom of the seas had become acceptable only by conceding to States wide powers over an area of sea adjacent to their coasts. And there were not lacking jurists who pointed out that a State would be even more concerned about what might take place in the air above it than in the seas off its coasts.

Fauchille proposed to meet this problem by conceding to the subjacent State extensive rights in the air space immediately above it. These rights would not be rights of territorial sovereignty but rights deriving ultimately from the principle of self-preservation.

Thus, in Articles 8 to 11 of his code, he would forbid navigation by foreign aircraft at heights of less than 1500 metres above national territory or at distances of less than 1500 metres from the coast. This distance was chosen for the practical reason that it was believed that 1500 metres was the maximum range at which worthwhile photographs of fortifications could be taken. In Article 15 Fauchille suggested that, in general, crimes committed on board foreign aircraft should be within the jurisdiction of the State of the aircraft, but that the subjacent State could punish crimes such as espionage and breaches of its customs and sanitary regulations, when committed in the air space above its territory. Such punishment would, however, be based on the protective rather than the territorial principle of jurisdiction because, according to Fauchille, the superjacent air space was 'free' and did not form part of the territory of the State.

This theory of the 'free air' died hard. It seems strange to us today that it should have been so strongly held. It may help to see things in perspective if we recall that the same view was widely taken in regard to territorial waters. We saw earlier that, in 1878, the British Parliament, reversing *The Queen* v. *Keyn*, asserted that British territorial waters were 'such part of the sea adjacent to the coast . . . as is deemed by international law to be within the territorial sovereignty of Her Majesty'. Yet, as late as 1921, it was held by the German Reichsgericht that German territorial waters were not, strictly speaking, part of German territory,[1] and as late as 1939 the Civil Tribunal of Brest took the same view of French territorial waters.[2]

One reason for the tenacity with which the 'free air' theory was held was undoubtedly the feeling that it was associated with the 'freedom of the seas', which had proved so beneficent a concept during the last three hundred years. Had not the Roman jurist, Celsus, asserted 'Maris communem usum omnibus hominibus ut aeris'? Moreover, had not Grotius himself, after basing the principle of the freedom of the seas on the argument that 'the extent of the ocean is in fact so great that it suffices for any possible use on the part of all people . . . ', gone on to say:

> The same thing would need to be said, too, about the air, if it were capable of any use for which the use of the land also is not required, as it is for the catching of birds. Fowling, therefore, and similar pursuits, are subject to the law laid down by him who has control over the land.[3]

We may note here the germ of a concept as far removed as could be from the doctrine of the freedom of the air. So long as the air is used for purposes 'for which the use of the land also is not required' it may be free. But, once the landowner is in some way concerned, then the use of the air becomes 'subject to the law laid down by him who has control over the land'. This leads us to consider the well-known maxim *Cujus est solum, ejus est usque ad coelum et ad inferos* which has figured so prominently in the literature of air law.

According to Lord McNair, the maxim itself is not Roman, but 'the tyranny' which it has exercised in England 'seems to be attributable in part to the traditional respect which English lawyers, while rejecting the complete *corpus juris civilis*, habitually show to what they conceive to be a rule of Roman law when it happens to accord with their own ideas, and in part to the grandiloquent manner adopted by English lawyers, notably Coke and Blackstone, in exalting the extent and importance of property in land'.[4]

Coke and Blackstone both cited the maxim, the former saying ' . . . the earth hath in law a great extent upwards, not only of water, as hath been said, but of ayre and of all other things even up to

---

[1] Territorial Waters Case. *Annual Digest and Reports of Public International Law Cases*, 1919–22, Case No. 63.

[2] *Compagnie Française des Câbles Télégraphiques* v. *Administration Française des Douanes. Annual Digest and Reports of Public International Law Cases*, 1938–40, Case No. 48.

[3] *De Juri Belli ac Pacis* (1625), Bk. II, Ch. 2, Section 3(1).

[4] *The Law of the Air* (3rd ed. 1964), p. 393.

heaven'[1] and the latter commenting 'the word "land" is not only the face of the earth but everything under it or *over it*'. Moreover, Blackstone also added: 'Land hath also, in its legal signification, *an indefinite extent upwards* as well as downwards.'[2]

We did not need to wait for the space age for the inconvenience of these doctrines to become apparent. In 1815 the case of *Pickering* v. *Rudd*[3] came before Lord Ellenborough. The case concerned an action for trespass *quare clausum fregit* arising out of the nailing upon the defendant's house of a board which projected over the plaintiff's garden. The learned Lord Chief Justice said:

I do not think it is a trespass to interfere with the column of air superincumbent on the close. I once had occasion to rule . . . that a man who, from the outside of a field, discharged a gun into it, so as that the shot must have struck the soil, was guilty of breaking and entering it. . . . But I am by no means prepared to say, that firing across a field *in vacuo*, no part of the contents touching it, amounts to a *clausum fregit*. Nay, if this board overhanging the plaintiff's garden be a trespass, it would follow that an aeronaut is liable to an action of trespass *quare clausum fregit* at the suit of the occupier of every field over which his balloon passes in the course of his voyage. . . . If any damage arises from the object which overhangs the close, the remedy is by an action on the case.

In *Kenyon* v. *Hart* (1865),[4] a case concerning trespass to game, Blackburn, J., referring to another case cited by counsel, said: 'That case raises the old query of Lord Ellenborough as to a man passing over the land of another in a balloon; he doubted whether an action of trespass would lie for it. I understand the good sense of that doubt, though not the legal reason of it.'

However, even before statute took a hand, the good sense of the common law shrank from the idea of regarding every invasion of air space above an owner's land as an actionable trespass, preferring to give the landowner the protection he undoubtedly needs through the more flexible action for nuisance, the essence of this tort being unreasonable interference with the plaintiff's use or enjoyment of his land.

In the United States, because of the great scale upon which aviation is conducted in that country and also because of the large number of jurisdictions that exist under their federal system of government, the courts have had more opportunity than the British courts to consider the status of the air space. It is convenient to mention a few decisions here even though they are more recent than the period we have been considering. In the *United States* v. *Causby*[5] the Supreme Court of

[1] Co. Litt. 4a. [2] Commentaries, Vol. II, Ch. 2, p. 18. Italics added.
[3] 4 Camp. 219. [4] 6 B and S 249. [5] (1946) 328 U.S. 256.

the United States held that the Government, by low flights of its military aircraft over a chicken farm, had 'taken' an easement of flight over the farm for which compensation must be paid. At the same time on the general issue the Court was cautious. It said:

It is ancient doctrine that at common law ownership of the land extended to the periphery of the universe—*Cujus est solum ejus est usque ad coelum*. But that doctrine has no place in the modern world. The air is a public highway . . . were that not true, every transcontinental flight would subject the operator to countless trespass suits. Common sense revolts at the idea.

The Court proceeded to hold that 'Flights over private land are not a taking, unless they are so low and so frequent as to be a direct and immediate interference with the enjoyment and use of the land.' But if, said the Court, 'by reason of the frequency and altitude of the flights, respondents could not use this land for any purpose, their loss would be complete. It would be as complete as if the United States had entered upon the surface of the land and taken exclusive possession of it.'

In *Griggs* v. *County of Allegheny*[1] the Supreme Court of the United States carried this doctrine further, holding that the operators of Greater Pittsburgh Airport had 'taken' an air easement over the property of a resident in the neighbourhood. In *Smith* v. *New England Aircraft Co.*,[2] the Supreme Judicial Court of Massachusetts considered more directly the question whether low flights across an owner's land constituted a trespass. It held that 'private ownership of airspace extends to all reasonable heights above the underlying land' and therefore that, 'after making every reasonable legal concession to air navigation', very low flights could amount to trespass.

In *Swetland* v. *Curtiss Airports Corporation*,[3] the United States Court of Appeals, Sixth Circuit, rejected the view that all decisions concerning air space must be decided upon the theory of nuisance rather than that of trespass. In a balanced judgement it said:

We cannot hold that in every case it is a trespass against the owner of the soil to fly an aeroplane through the air space overlying the surface. This does not mean that the owner of the surface has no right at all in the air space above his land. He has a dominant right of occupancy for purposes incident to his use and enjoyment of the surface, and there may be such a continuous and permanent use of the lower stratum which he may reasonably expect to use or occupy himself as to impose a servitude upon

---

[1] (1962) 369 U.S. 84. [2] (1930) 270 Mass. 511, 170 N.E. 385.
[3] (1932) 55 F. 2d. 201.

his use and enjoyment of the surface.[1] As to the upper stratum which he may not reasonably expect to occupy, he has no right . . . except to prevent the use of it by others to the extent of an unreasonable interference with his complete enjoyment of the surface. His remedy for this latter use . . . is an action for nuisance and not trespass.

The relevance to international air law of these decisions may be questioned, even though in one of them, *Smith* v. *New England Aircraft Co.*, the tribunal, referring to the international aspect, said: 'It is essential to the safety of sovereign States that they possess jurisdiction to control the air space above their territories. It seems to us to rest on the obvious practical necessity of self-protection. Every government completely sovereign in character must possess power to prevent from entering its confines those whom it determines to be undesirable.' This short passage is interesting because it looks as if the court felt able to base the right of a State to control its air space on both the theory of territorial sovereignty and the theory of self-protection, without troubling too much about the controversies among international jurists as to which of these two theories is the proper basis. Moreover, even if these international jurists had agreed that the air was in principle 'free', and even if States had been prepared to accept the presence of foreign aviators in their air space, it would have availed such aviators little if they had then found themselves sued in private actions by every landowner above whose land they had happened to fly.

It must be remembered too that 'the general principles of law recognized by civilized nations' constitute an important source of international law, the more so when treaties and customary rules are lacking;[2] and that there is as yet no agreed limit for the boundary between national air space and 'outer space'. Consequently, the experience of the common law courts in applying the ancient notions of trespass and nuisance to activities in the air space above the land of private owners may yet provide a basis for developing a sound jurisprudence for the 'aerospace law' of the future.

[1] E.g., extensive low flying, as was alleged in this case.
[2] See Article 38(1) of the Statute of the International Court of Justice.

Chapter II

THE PERIOD FROM 1903 TO 1914

THE MILITARY SIDE

IN 1907, at the Second Hague Peace Conference, the question arose of renewing the 1899 Declaration prohibiting the discharge of projectiles and explosives from balloons, which had expired in 1905. It was agreed to renew the Declaration 'for a period extending to the close of the Third Peace Conference' which was expected to be held in 1914. This time Great Britain was among the seventeen countries which ratified or adhered to the Declaration, but otherwise the Declaration received little support from the great European Powers. Thus, Italy, who had not ratified the Declaration, considered herself to be within her legal rights in dropping bombs from balloons in her war against Turkey in 1911.

It remains then to consider what was the legal position as regards Powers not bound by the Declaration. Article 25 of the Regulations annexed to Convention (II) with respect to the Laws and Customs of War on Land, signed at The Hague on 29 July 1899, provided as follows:

> The attack or bombardment of towns, villages, habitations or buildings, which are not defended, is prohibited.

In the Regulations annexed to the corresponding Convention (IV), signed at The Hague on 18 October 1907, the words 'by any means whatever' were added to this Regulation. This Convention received a large number of ratifications and has come to be regarded as generally declaratory of the laws of war on land. There can be no doubt that the aim of the additional words was to prevent the bombardment from the air of undefended 'villages, towns, habitations or buildings', and it was for this reason that various proposals for strengthening the Declaration of 1899 were not proceeded with. Moreover, Article 26 of the same Regulations (both the 1899 version and the 1907 version) required the commander of an attacking force, before commencing a bombardment, except in the case of an assault, to do all he could to warn the authorities. Should a bombardment take place,

Article 27 (both versions) stated that all necessary steps were to be taken to spare as far as possible buildings dedicated to religion, art, science, hospitals, etc. 'provided they are not being used at the same time for military purposes'.

At the same time we must note that the provisions of Convention (IX), concerning Bombardment by Naval Forces in Time of War, likewise signed at The Hague on 18 October 1907, were less exacting. This Convention, while stating as a general principle that the bombardment by naval forces of undefended ports, towns, villages, dwellings or buildings was forbidden, permitted such bombardment in the case of 'military works, military or naval establishments, depots of arms or war material, workshops or plant which could be utilized for the needs of the hostile fleet or army, and ships of war in the harbour'—even if these targets were in undefended towns. The naval commander was normally required to give notice, but he was exempted from 'responsibility for any unavoidable damage which may be caused by a bombardment under such circumstances'. Bombardment of undefended places was also permitted in case of a refusal to comply with requisitions for provisions or supplies necessary for the immediate use of the naval force concerned, although in any bombardment by naval forces care had to be taken to spare as far as possible buildings devoted to public worship, art, science or charitable purposes, historic monuments and hospitals.

There was thus the following progress, or rather regression, in the law. According to Article 15 of the unratified Brussels Declaration (1874), only 'fortified places' were liable to be besieged, and 'towns, agglomerations of houses or open villages, which are undefended' were not to be attacked or bombarded at all. Article 25 of the Hague Regulations of 1899 was slightly weaker in that the specific and contrasting references to 'fortified places', which could be attacked, and 'open villages', which could not, did not appear. This article was tightened up in 1907 by the inclusion of the words 'by any means whatever' in the provision forbidding the bombardment of undefended places. At the same time, however, a wide liberty was given to naval forces to bombard even undefended places so long as they directed their attack against military objectives.

In view of later developments, it may be as well to draw attention to two features of the law as it thus stood in 1907:

(i) The reason for the greater freedom of naval bombardment was that it was realized that the commander of a naval force, unlike his opposite number on land, was not in a position to take possession of an undefended place. Unlike land warfare, which was conceived of as taking place in a relatively determinate zone of operations, naval forces by virtue of their greater mobility were regarded as taking the theatre of war around with them.

(ii) The corollary of the restrictions on bombardment of an undefended place in land warfare was that, in the case of a defended place, the bombardment would be unrestricted save for the injunction, stated in Article 27 of the Hague Regulations, to spare certain edifices 'as far as possible'.

It is easy to see here, that, quite apart from any question of reprisals, there were two loopholes which belligerent air forces might employ to justify a fairly liberal policy of bombardment. First, they could invoke their inability to take possession of the places they wanted to attack, as well as their general mobility, and claim the same privileges as naval forces. Secondly, they could argue that the places they wanted to attack were in one way or another defended.

It was obvious at the time that, having regard to the historic differences between land war and naval war, the framing of suitable regulations for air warfare was going to be a matter of great difficulty. Apart from the variation in the rules relating to bombardment to which I have already drawn attention, there were the following major differences. Land war rules emphasize the importance of *uniform* as the means of distinguishing combatants from non-combatants, whereas sea war rules lay stress on the nature of the *vessel* and the *flag* it flies. Sea war rules are far less strict than land war rules about ruses, such as the wearing of false colours. By contrast, sea war rules permit the capture of private property, whereas land war rules normally do not. Finally, whereas in land war a neutral is expected to take the strictest measures to prevent the use of his territory by belligerent troops, in sea war a State's neutrality is not compromised by the mere passage through its territorial waters of belligerent warships. Indeed a neutral State may even admit such ships to its ports, provided that the privilege is granted impartially and is not abused.

There were a number of possible solutions to the problem of laying down basic rules for air warfare. The rules of land war could be applied *en bloc* to air forces, wherever these forces fought. Alternatively, the rules of naval war could be applied to the air forces *en bloc* wherever they fought. Another possibility would be to say that the air forces must conform to the rules of land or sea war depending upon the operation in which they happened to be engaged. It is obvious that all these solutions were attended with disadvantages. So it is not surprising that no major attempt at codification was made. 'Balloons and flying machines' were, however, treated as conditional contraband of war under the Declaration of London (1909) which, although it never came to be ratified, purported to state 'generally recognized principles of international law' in the general field of blockade, contraband and unneutral service.

THE CIVIL SIDE

In 1906, the Institute of International Law, meeting in Ghent, generally endorsed the views put forward four years earlier by Fauchille. In so doing, the Institute rejected the more extreme views of the Belgian writer, Nys, who wanted a more complete freedom of the air. Likewise it rejected the approach of the English authority, Westlake, who wanted the subjacent State to have sovereignty over the air space, subject to a right of innocent passage for foreign aircraft. Four years later, however, Fauchille somewhat modified his own views. This time, reporting to the Institute for its Paris session (1910), he proposed merely to say 'La circulation aérienne est libre', thus leaving open the status of the air space as such. He also endeavoured to tackle in a different way the problem of photography from the air. Taking into account the improvement in photographic techniques, as also the changes in aviation consequent upon the development of aeroplanes alongside airships, he proposed to separate altogether the question of flight altitudes and the question of espionage by camera. He would allow foreign aircraft to fly as low as 500 metres, which he considered a sufficient height for safety purposes, and he would forbid altogether the carrying of photographic apparatus.

In 1911, meeting in Madrid, the Institute fell in with this approach. Two years later, also meeting in Madrid, the International Law Association adopted a resolution which, while still paying lip service to the principle of freedom of aerial navigation, asserted very much more strongly the powers of the subjacent State. This resolution read as follows:

1. It is the right of every State to enact such prohibitions, restrictions, and regulations as it may think proper in regard to the passage of aircraft through the air space above its territories and territorial waters.

2. Subject to this right of subjacent States, liberty of passage of aircraft ought to be accorded freely to the aircraft of every nation.

This change in the attitude of private bodies interested in air law only reflected the growing concern of Governments. Thus in 1911 the British Parliament passed the Aerial Navigation Act in which it enacted that 'a Secretary of State may, for the purpose of protecting the public from danger, from time to time by order prohibit the navigation of aircraft over such areas as may be prescribed in the order'. The Act had a limited purpose, namely the prevention of accidents during the Coronation procession of that year, but the Aerial Navigation Act of 1913 was drafted in much broader terms. This empowered a Secretary of State to prohibit the navigation of aircraft over any areas prescribed for him for a number of purposes, including the 'defence or safety of the realm'; authorized firing at aircraft which failed to comply; and stated that the prescribed areas 'may include the whole or any part of the coastline of the United Kingdom and the territorial waters adjacent thereto'. Whatever might have been thought of the Act of 1911, the Act of 1913 was therefore a clear assertion of national sovereignty in air space.

Nor were there lacking writers who discerned the signs of the times. Giving a series of lectures at King's College, London, in 1910, Mr. H. D. Hazeltine, an American who was then Reader in English Law in the University of Cambridge, took issue with those who thought that the status of the air space was not an urgent problem. 'I believe', he said, 'that the proper settlement of the question as to what rights States have in the column of air above their territory is of first and fundamental importance.'[1] Contrasting theories which advocated some kind of 'freedom of the air' with theories which stressed the sovereignty of the subjacent State over its air space, Hazeltine came out strongly in favour of the latter. He took the view that States were already claiming such sovereignty. Nor, in his view, would it be necessary to grant a right of innocent passage for foreign aircraft. As he rather optimistically put it:[2]

Just as States have welcomed and adopted the principle of internationalism as regards sea navigation in territorial waters, international railway and motor traffic on land, international wireless communication,

---

[1] *The Law of the Air* (1911), p. 8. It is interesting that, forty years later, the United Nations *Ad Hoc* Committee on the Peaceful Uses of Outer Space reported that 'It was generally believed that the determination of precise limits for air space and outer space did not present a legal problem calling for priority consideration at this moment' (U.N. Document A/4141, 14 July 1959, paragraph 28). There is, however, no more unanimity among jurists today on this question than there was on the corresponding question in 1910.

[2] Op. cit., pp. 51–2.

and admission of aliens to the enjoyment of the laws and privileges of the territorial State, so, too, the self-interest of States will naturally lead them to welcome and develop this new method of navigation along international as well as national lines.

Lecturing in the University of Oxford in 1912,[1] Sir Erle Richards, Professor of International Law in that University, claimed that the rights of States over the air were 'already fixed and determined by admitted principles of International Law'. Conceding that there was no convention on air law, Richards nevertheless said: 'In my judgement the matter is covered, or, as I would rather say, is concluded, by a principle of International Law which is fundamental in the determination of the extent of State sovereignty and must apply as much to the air space above State Territory as to the Territory itself. This principle is that Sovereign States are entitled to all those rights which are necessary for the preservation and protection of their territories.' In Richards' view, sovereignty over the superjacent air space was even more essential for this purpose than was sovereignty over territorial waters. 'The bed-rock fact', he said, 'is that the user of the air cannot be treated as a thing distinct from the user of the territory beneath it; the two are inseparably connected, and can never be dissociated until the law of gravity ceases to have effect.' Again stressing the law of gravity, Richards rejected as inapplicable to air law the customary right of innocent passage enjoyed by merchant shipping. But one argument he used to reject that right—the statement that 'the air vessel cannot make prolonged flights without landing'—clearly has no validity today.

The practice of States has in the main endorsed these views of Hazeltine and Richards. But the position was hardly as clear-cut as they seemed to imagine. That there was no international convention at the time that Richards spoke was due to a failure to reach agreement at the Paris Conference of 1910 (attended by the representatives of nineteen States) on the very point which he thought was self-evident. At this Conference the British Government unequivocally supported the sovereignty theory. It would not even allow that foreign aircraft had a right of innocent passage. The French and German Governments were more ready to pay lip-service to the freedom of the air, but their proposals did not differ greatly in practice from those of the British Government which was in fact prepared to grant certain rights of flight to foreign aircraft under the proposed convention. Some difficulty was experienced over the

[1] *Sovereignty over the Air* (1912), pp. 4–9, 14–16.

consequential adjustments to municipal law that would be required as a result of granting to foreign aircraft these rights of flight. But the real cause of the breakdown appears to have been disagreement over the extent to which, on security grounds, States could refrain from giving to foreign aircraft the same rights of aerial navigation as they gave to their own aircraft.

The devotion of the French and German Governments to the freedom of the air was revealed to be somewhat half-hearted when on 26 July 1913, they arrived at an exchange of notes in which, 'en attendant la conclusion d'une convention sur cette matière entre un plus grand nombre d'Etats', they decided 'd'une manière provisoire et à charge de reciprocité' to admit to each other's territory aircraft coming from the other. The agreement was, in fact, hedged around with all manner of security restrictions. Even so, it is entitled to an important place in the history of air law because it was the forerunner of innumerable bilateral agreements in which the Government of one country opened its skies to a certain extent to the aircraft of another.

As we shall see, in later lectures, air law has been developed, and has reached the relatively advanced position that it enjoys today, thanks to a combination of multilateral and bilateral agreements. Later experience has tended to confirm the early lesson that agreement on aeronautical questions between large numbers of States is not easy to achieve; and that, in so far as it can be achieved, the range of matters agreed upon is likely to be limited. Even so the Conference of 1910 was not a total failure. It prepared a draft convention which was much influenced by the preparatory studies of Fauchille and the Institute of International Law. In its turn this draft convention came in useful when the Versailles Peace Conference took up the same problem nine years later. Among some of the provisions of the 1910 draft were the following: It insisted that aircraft (the term now used was *aéronefs*, no longer *aérostats*) in order to enjoy rights under the convention, possess the nationality of a contracting State (Article 2). Subject to certain restrictions, it would be for each State to decide the exact basis on which it would grant such nationality (Article 3). Dual nationality would be forbidden (Article 4). Nationality would be indicated by inscribing the aircraft on a register (Article 6). Registered aircraft would be provided with certificates (Article 8). In order to enjoy the right of navigation above the territory of other contracting States, aircraft must carry the appropriate nationality mark and registration number (Article 10).

Aircraft must also have certificates of airworthiness issued by the appropriate national authorities (Articles 11–13). Similarly the pilot and crew must have the necessary certificates of competence issued by the same authorities (Article 14). Provided these certificates were granted according to the conditions laid down in the convention, other contracting States would recognize them (Article 18). Regulations along these general lines are to be found in virtually all international aviation agreements that have been concluded subsequently.

Chapter III

THE FIRST WORLD WAR, THE PARIS CONVENTION AND THE HAGUE AIR WARFARE RULES

THE FIRST WORLD WAR

WHEN the First World War broke out, Great Britain had twelve military aircraft; she finished the war with twenty-two thousand. Such is the scale of the developments we have now to consider. In 1914 the military role of aircraft was uncertain. Reconnaissance seemed to be the task on which aeroplanes would most probably be engaged, whilst balloons would continue to be used to assist artillery. At first aircraft were unarmed, save for the personal arms of the aviators, and aerial combats were not envisaged. But it was not long before the problems involved in fitting machine-guns to aeroplanes and firing them through propellers were overcome. The search then began for an effective method of shooting down observation balloons because ordinary machine-gun bullets simply went through the gas-bag, doing little harm. Cannon were tried, but without success. In 1916, however, the problem was solved through the invention by the Allies of an incendiary bullet. This bullet almost certainly contravened the provisions of the St. Petersburg Declaration, and also those of a Hague Declaration of 1899 which forbade the use of bullets 'which expand or flatten easily in the human body . . .' Nevertheless, the bullets proved so efficient for the purposes for which they were designed that they were soon widely used by both sides, although, in order to avoid liability for war crimes, it remained the practice to issue airmen with certificates authorizing their use against balloons only.

It also became the practice for airmen to use tracer bullets. These are ordinary machine-gun bullets with incandescent material at the base. They are intended not to set targets on fire but to enable the firer to observe the path of the bullet. It seems that occasionally aeroplanes and even observation balloons were set on fire by such bullets, but that was not their purpose or normal effect. Bullets of

26

this type were employed by ground forces also, and it was not considered that their use amounted to a breach of the St. Petersburg Declaration.

Success in shooting down observation balloons gave rise to another problem. Could the observers be shot as they descended by parachute (this being incidentally the first use to which parachutes were put)? Again, by the rude practice of war, the answer proved to be in the affirmative, the military reason being that it was considered more important to destroy the observer than the balloon.

By 'the rude practice of war' I mean simply what the belligerents did. So long as what is done in war is done consistently, by both sides, with an absence of protest and without excessive reliance on the doctrine of reprisals—about which I shall soon have something to say—this 'rude practice' is as good a method as any of developing the customary laws of warfare. It sometimes works better than the method of drawing up conventions in peacetime, because such conventions are apt to be prepared against a background of pressures which have little to do with the realities of war.

Although it had been tried out in the Italo-Turkish war, bombing was approached by the protagonists in the Great War with some caution. Allied practice was ostensibly to follow the naval rule and confine bombing attacks to military objectives, without troubling whether the towns attacked were defended or not. Germany, on the other hand, claimed to follow a policy of bombing only places within the actual theatre of war, but this operational zone was interpreted flexibly. Thus London was claimed to be in the zone of operations, while German cities were not.

Lecturing at Oxford in 1915, Sir Erle Richards strongly contested the legality of the German air raids, arguing that such raids were not permissible unless they had a direct military purpose such as the capture of a town. In his view, even a defended town—if London could be said to be a defended town—could not be attacked unless its surrender were demanded by military forces and refused.

Such was also apparently the British Government's view at the time. On 15 September 1915, defending the Government against accusations that insufficient had been done to defend London against air raids, Mr. Balfour, First Lord of the Admiralty, gave a curious answer. He said:

If the right honourable Gentleman asks me whether I think that at this moment everything has been done that could be done, or will be done, for the defence of London, I do not think so. I think the thing is still in progress, and still in process of development. If he asks me whether I think it possible, within a reasonable time, to provide an adequate defence of London, I should give him a much reassuring answer. . . . The right honourable Gentleman mentioned Paris. Well, Sir, pains have been taken to make ourselves acquainted with the methods of the defence of Paris, and much no doubt has been learned, and will be learned, from studying their example. But let not the House be carried away with the idea that the problem of London is identical with the problem of Paris. . . . Paris starts with being under a single military government, and it starts with being a great military fortress therefore, being a military fortress, it is supplied with a great mass of guns and with great defensive arrangements. London is not a fortified town. London is, as everybody knows—nobody knows it better than the Germans—a city which should not, under the law of civilized warfare, be the subject of this kind of attack. But we take our enemies as we find them.[1]

In this answer Mr. Balfour admitted that London was a badly defended town, but in the light of his pledge to improve its defences he could hardly pretend that it was an undefended town. On what then did he rest London's claim to immunity from bombardment, as distinct from Paris? Presumably on the consideration that London was further removed from the front than was Paris and that the Channel moat was there to prevent the Germans from capturing it by a sudden thrust. But, save at certain grim stages of the war, Paris was hardly within the immediate zone of operations. Moreover, even if the improbability of direct military capture had been a sufficient criterion of immunity from aerial bombardment in the First World War, this test would have had little validity in the subsequent conflict when the capture of cities by parachutists and glider-borne troops became a regular military stratagem.

Naturally British public opinion, ignoring such niceties, looked upon all German air raids as wanton attacks on civilians and consequently criminal. At various stages of the war (notably October 1915, January 1916, and May 1917) the correspondence columns of *The Times* were filled with letters demanding 'reprisals'. Legal opinion, as expressed through such personalities as Lord Alverstone and Sir Edward Clarke (both former Law Officers), Lord Bryce and Professor A. V. Dicey, was generally opposed to a policy of indiscriminate retaliation, although in a letter published on 7 May 1917, Sir Thomas Holland, Richards' predecessor at Oxford, frankly assuming that the British raid on Freiburg of 14 April of that year was 'deliberately intended to result in injury to the property and persons of civilian inhabitants, not, of course, by way of vengeance,

[1] *Parliamentary Debates, Commons* (1914–15), Vol. 74, Col. 70.

but by way of reprisal', was no less prepared frankly to justify it as such.

The Freiburg raid was debated in the House of Lords on 2 May. Opening the debate the Archbishop of Canterbury referred to a resolution just passed by the Upper House of Convocation of Canterbury which, confirming an earlier resolution, said '... the principles of morality forbid a policy of reprisal which has, as a deliberate object, the killing and wounding of non-combatants'. Justifying the raid, Earl Curzon of Kedleston, Lord President of the Council, explained that it had been decided upon as a reprisal, not for German air raids, but for deliberate sinkings by the enemy of British hospital ships. The Germans had announced earlier in the year their intention to sink such ships, and the British Government for their part had intimated to the enemy their resolve to take measures of reprisal should the Germans so act. He also claimed, however, that Freiburg was a defended town—a claim which, if true, would have gone part, if not all, of the way towards justifying the raid in itself. But Earl Curzon did not claim that military objectives were aimed at, and he even implied that they were not. When his turn came to speak for the Government, Viscount Milner (Minister without Portfolio) was asked to say whether or not the object of the raid was to injure civilian people and civilian property. When he answered that the object was to prevent British soldiers and nurses being drowned, he was told by Lord Buckmaster, who had asked the question, that that was not the object of the raid but its motive. At this point, Viscount Milner prevaricated, but proceeded to admit that a town could not be bombed without injuring civilians and their property. But he finally insisted that there was no other way of checking the German outrages 'besides of ourselves doing an act beyond the ordinary practices of civilian warfare as we have always followed it'.[1] The whole debate reveals an extraordinary schizophrenia on the part of the Government spokesmen whether, without the element of reprisal, the raid would have been justified or not.

In general, in international law, reprisals are measures which in normal circumstances would be illegal, but which a State may lawfully take for the purpose of compelling another State to remedy a wrong. Under the laws of war, in particular, they are illegal acts of warfare authorized for the purpose of compelling the other belligerent to comply with rules of war which he has been violating. They serve a

[1] *Parliamentary Debates, Lords* (1917), Vol. 24, Cols. 1013–38.

purpose, but are no less liable to abuse. In the First World War considerable and unnecessary confusion was caused by the demand of public opinion for 'reprisals' after almost all raids, and correspondingly for Governments to designate as 'reprisals' raids which were perhaps lawful in themselves. As we saw in the case of the debate on the Freiburg raid, however, Governments harmed themselves in so doing because the consequence of announcing that something had been done as a reprisal sometimes was that an event which might otherwise have passed unnoticed as an ordinary incident of war provoked an unwelcome controversy on the wider question as to whether retaliatory action involving deliberate breaches of the laws of war was justified or not. This does not of course answer the question what was a 'lawful raid'. Here again the 'rude practice of war' is our best guide. There is very little evidence that any of the belligerents in the 1914–18 war adopted as a sustained policy the making of what in the Second World War became known as 'terror raids'. But that is not to say that the damage done to civilian lives and property even in the first conflict was inconsiderable, or that the potentiality of air raids as a weapon of psychological warfare was not appreciated. Equally it would be unwise to assume that the belligerents abstained from aerial attacks deliberately aimed at civilians solely out of a sense of moral, let alone legal, obligations. Powerful as was the tradition that non-combatants should as far as possible be spared the horrors of war, it collapsed altogether in the war at sea under the double impact of the German submarine campaign and the Allied counter-measures in the matter of blockade and contraband control. Here unfortunately was a case where the introduction of a new weapon had produced a situation for which the laws of war were hopelessly unprepared. What was true of the submarine was also to a large extent true of the aeroplane.

The fear of a riposte by the enemy, however, was one motive which restrained belligerent ardour in the matter of air raids. Another motive, possibly even more powerful, was the purely military consideration that the mounting of raids involved a serious diversion of effort. Indeed the view was widely held that the main value of raids lay not so much in the damage done as in the fact that one belligerent was compelled to divert even more resources to defending cities than the other was to attacking them. War being what it is, it was possible for this view to be held, and acted upon, by both sides. Nevertheless, even though civilians were not as a rule deliberately attacked, there were some Ministers who had no illusions about air raids. As early as 5 September 1914, Mr. (as he then was) Winston Churchill, Balfour's predecessor at the Admiralty, wrote a minute on the subject of preparing the civil population for aerial bombardment. 'This', he said in his characteristic style, 'will have to be sustained with composure.'[1] A revealing incident took place in the House of Commons on 21 February 1918. Mr. J. King (M.P. for Somerset, North) moved an Amendment to the Air Force estimates, in which he proposed to add the words 'air attacks against the enemy should be carried out with military objectives and in such a manner as to avoid, as far as possible, injury to non-combatants, women and children'. Replying, Major Baird, Under-Secretary of State at the Air Ministry, said: 'We are at war, and everything that we are doing has a military objective. . . . Do not let us bandy words. It is impossible to drop bombs on any towns—German, French or English —without running the risk of killing women and children.'[2]

Two cases involving bombing in the First World War were subsequently referred to the Greco–German Mixed Arbitral Tribunal. In the first of these, *Coenca Brothers* v. *Germany*,[3] the Tribunal held that a German air raid on Salonica was 'contrary to international law' because of the failure to give the warning required by Article 26 of the Hague Regulations (1907). In the next case, *Kiriadolou* v. *Germany*,[4] the Tribunal arrived at a similar conclusion in regard to an air attack on Bucharest. In the *Coenca Bros.* case, the Tribunal admitted that Article 26 of the Hague Regulations envisaged only land bombardment. 'However', the Tribunal went on, 'it was generally recognized that there was no reason why the rule as to land bombardment should not apply to bombardment from the air. The argument of the defendant State that bombardment from the air must necessarily be a surprise attack may be correct from the military point of view, but this does not imply that bombardment without warning ought to be permitted. On the contrary, the implication would be that such bombardment is generally inadmissible.' Further in the *Kiriadolou* case, the Tribunal said:

The distinction between bombardment for occupation and bombardment for destruction has no juridical basis and cannot absolve air forces from the duty to give preliminary notification. This is the more so since an air-plane, which very frequently flies by night over the town threatened

[1] *The World Crisis, 1911–1914*, p. 316. London, Thornton Butterworth Ltd.
[2] *Parliamentary Debates, Commons* (1918), Vol. 103, Cols. 1065–6.
[3] *Annual Digest and Reports of Public International Law Cases*, 1927–8. Case No. 389.
[4] Ibid., 1929–30. Case No. 301.

by bombardment at an altitude of several thousand metres, is not in a position to direct with precision the fall of bombs so as to ensure that they hit only the fortifications and war munitions, without harm being done to the persons and the property of non-combatants.

It is difficult to know what attitude to take towards these brave, but isolated, decisions. It is possible to admire the determination to maintain the distinction between combatants and non-combatants; to apply literally the provisions of the Hague Regulations; and to make the minimum of concessions to the necessities of war. On the other hand, the laws of war rest upon a reasonable compromise between the standards of civilization and these selfsame necessities of war. It was surely unrealistic of the Tribunal to ignore the fact that only on very rare and special occasions was it the practice of any of the belligerents to give advance notification of air raids. Moreover, the assertion that 'the distinction between bombardment for occupation and bombardment for destruction has no juridical basis' is patently untrue if one takes the Ninth Hague Convention into account. In retrospect, it seems that perfectionist decisions of this sort made it more difficult to work out an effective code of air warfare.

If the First World War left many legal issues undecided, it did appear to settle one question beyond dispute. This was the status of the air space, a matter which had given rise to so much theoretical discussion before the conflict. As early as 3 August 1914, the Netherlands Government prohibited flights above their territory. The Swiss Government followed suit five days later, and other neutrals did the same. Sometimes neutral countries enforced these prohibitions by gunfire, no exceptions being made as a rule for cases of navigational error or even distress. On the whole, belligerents accepted the right of neutrals to take this firm action although, in a note addressed to Switzerland in 1914, following upon a violation of Swiss territory by British aircraft during a raid on Friedrichshafen, the British Government, while expressing regret at the violation, also stated that their regret was not to be interpreted as the recognition by them of any sovereignty over the air.

So early and so firmly was the right, and even the duty, of neutrals to protect their air space against violation established that, in his 1915 Oxford lecture, Sir Erle Richards was able to say:

The practice of the present war seems definitely to have established the right of every State to sovereignty over the air space above its territories. There has been some diversity of opinion on this point and it may be within the recollection of the members of the university that, on a former occasion,

I had the honour of addressing them upon it. In the present war the claim to sovereignty has been continuously asserted by neutral States over whose territories belligerent aircraft have passed, and the claim has been sanctioned by acquiescence if not by express admission.

THE PARIS CONVENTION, 1919

When the war ended, an Aeronautical Commission was established to advise the Peace Conference at Versailles on all air matters and also to draft a convention for the general regulation of post-war international aviation. The Treaty of Versailles itself, signed on 28 June 1919, contained a number of articles aimed at preventing the restoration of Germany's air power. For example, Germany was forbidden to have military or naval air forces; and temporarily the aircraft of the Allied and Associated Powers were to have rights of passage, transit and landing in German territory. The same philosophy of discrimination against Germany dominated the Convention for the Regulation of Aerial Navigation agreed in Paris on 13 October 1919. In Article 1 of this Convention the High Contracting Parties recognized 'that every Power has complete and exclusive sovereignty over the air space above its territory'—territory for this purpose being defined as including adjacent territorial waters. This statement of historic significance in the evolution of air law was followed up in Article 2 by a provision to the effect that 'each contracting State undertakes in time of peace to accord freedom of innocent passage above its territory to the aircraft of the other contracting States, provided that the conditions laid down in the present Convention are observed'. Thus, whilst sovereignty over the air space above its territory was asserted as a right of all States under customary international law (except where expressly derogated from, as in certain provisions of the Treaty of Versailles), freedom of passage for foreign aircraft was set forth merely as a contractual right under the Convention, to which Germany was forbidden to become a party for the time being (Article 42). Further, under Article 3 of the Convention, contracting States were given the right 'for military reasons or in the interest of public safety' to prohibit the aircraft of the other contracting States from flying over certain areas of their territory, provided no discrimination was shown in favour of their own aircraft.

On the whole, however, the Convention was inspired by a liberal spirit. Following ideas already sketched out in Fauchille's code of 1902 and in the abortive draft convention of 1910, the scheme was that all aircraft should possess a nationality through being on the

33

register of a contracting State; that the State where the aircraft was registered should be responsible for issuing certificates of airworthiness to the aircraft and of certificates of competency and licences to the crew; that these certificates should be recognized as valid by the other contracting States; and that aircraft thus certificated should be permitted certain rights of flight in the territory of each contracting State. There were naturally certain restrictions. Apart from the prohibited areas already mentioned, each contracting State was given the 'right to establish reservations and restrictions in favour of its national aircraft in connection with the carriage of persons and goods for hire between two points on its territory' (Article 16). This was the so-called 'cabotage' right, named after the similar right which coastal States enjoy as regards maritime traffic. States were also given complete power to prohibit or regulate the carriage or use of photographic apparatus (Article 27). 'State aircraft', defined as (a) Military aircraft and (b) Aircraft exclusively employed in State service, such as posts, customs and police, were excluded from the scheme (Article 30). But aircraft engaged in commerce, even if owned by a State or by a State-supported corporation, were treated as 'private aircraft' and entitled to the benefits of the Convention—a most significant and progressive step. Finally, in case of war, the provisions of the Convention were not to affect the freedom of action of the contracting States, either as belligerents or as neutrals (Article 38).

There was also to be constituted an International Commission for Air Navigation (usually known as CINA after its French initials— 'Commission Internationale de Navigation Aérienne'), whose main task would be to keep up to date the technical provisions of the Convention. These were embodied in Annexes which were declared to have the same effect as the Convention itself (Article 39). Despite that fact, the Annexes (save for Annex H, which dealt with customs matters) could be amended by a qualified majority vote within the Commission. The latter was thus given limited quasi-legislative powers, a significant stage in the evolution of international institutions.

The greatest uncertainty surrounded the extent of the freedom of innocent passage granted under Article 2. This should have been cleared up by Article 15 which, however, only succeeded in complicating the situation. This article provided that 'every aircraft of a contracting State has the right to cross the air space of another State without landing'. Such aircraft were, however, required to follow the route fixed by the subjacent State and could 'for reasons of general security' be obliged to land. Moreover, all aircraft passing 'from one State into another' could be required to land at one of the aerodromes 'fixed by the latter'. Finally, and most ambiguously of all, it was provided that 'the establishment of international airways shall be subject to the consent of the States flown over'.

The latter provision, in the British view, was intended to refer to the navigational practice of aircraft flying regularly along a fixed route. However, it could be interpreted to mean that the establishment of a commercial route itself, operated by an airline company, should be made subject to the consent of the State flown over. This matter was argued about for many years, but finally, on 15 June 1929, at an extraordinary session of the International Commission for Air Navigation in Paris, an amendment was adopted stating definitely that the provision was to be understood in the latter restrictive sense, viz.:

Every contracting State may make conditional on its prior authorization the establishment of international airways and the creation and operation of regular international air navigation lines, with or without landing, on its territory.

By way of a concession to the British thesis, the Commission adopted also a resolution in which it decided to recommend to Governments not to refuse the authorization referred to 'otherwise than upon reasonable grounds'. Unfortunately this recommendation was not widely adhered to.

At the same meeting in 1929 the opportunity was taken to make Article 3 more restrictive in the sense that, if a State declared a prohibited area, it was now to be allowed 'as an exceptional measure and in the interest of public safety', to authorize flights over the area by its own national aircraft. A State was also to be allowed, 'in exceptional circumstances in time of peace and with immediate effect temporarily to restrict or prohibit flight over its territory or over part of its territory on condition that such restriction or prohibition shall be applicable without distinction of nationality to the aircraft of all the other States'. But while discrimination must be avoided as between 'all the other States', a State was, under this provision, too, entitled to reserve the right of flight to its own aircraft.

Ultimately thirty-eight States became parties to the Paris Convention. They included Great Britain and the Dominions, nineteen European States, eight Latin-American States, Iran, Iraq, Japan and

Siam. Significant absentees were Germany, the Soviet Union and the United States.

Despite its failure to guarantee effectively the right of flight, and despite the limited number of States that were parties to it, the Paris Convention, supplemented as it was by many bilateral agreements, provided a framework in which international civil aviation was able, if not to flourish, at least to expand between the two wars. In order to give effect to the Convention, the British Parliament passed the Air Navigation Act, 1920. Under Section 1 of this Act, power was conferred on His Majesty to make Orders in Council for the purpose of carrying out the Convention, including any amendments that might be made to it. Section 3 enumerated a long list of purposes connected with the control of air navigation for which Orders in Council might also be made, thus enabling the Acts of 1911 and 1913 to be repealed. Section 9 enacted the important principle that 'No action shall lie in respect of trespass or in respect of nuisance, by reason only of the flight of aircraft over any property at a height above the ground, which, having regard to wind, weather, and all the circumstances of the case is reasonable, or the ordinary incidents of such flight, so long as the provisions of this Act and any Order made thereunder and of the Convention are duly complied with'. The effect of this Section has been virtually to prevent the courts from having to deal with litigation of a type that has been fairly common in the United States. Although this has had some advantages, it has also been partly responsible for the relatively little interest taken in air law in this country. Finally, it is interesting to note that the Preamble of the 1920 Act, using words in some respects similar to those of the Territorial Waters Jurisdiction Act, 1878, asserts the following:

Whereas the full and absolute sovereignty and rightful jurisdiction of His Majesty extends, and has always extended, over the air superincumbent on all parts of His Majesty's dominions and the territorial waters adjacent thereto. . . .

In addition to the Paris Convention, a Convention was signed in Madrid in 1926 by Spain and a few Latin-American States, and another one in Havana in 1928 by the U.S.A. and rather more Latin-American States. Only seven States ratified the former Convention, and only sixteen the latter. Neither Convention resulted in the establishment of an organization as productive as CINA. At a time when the range of aircraft was limited, these regional Conventions played a useful, if limited, role in the elaboration of air law. It is useless to pretend, however, that aviation can be regulated satisfactorily otherwise than on a world basis. Fortunately, the division of the world into separate Convention areas did not prevent a coming together over what was, from the ordinary passenger's point of view, a most important matter. This was the question of the unification of the rules relating to international carriage by air, especially as regards the liability of carriers for 'damage sustained in the event of the death or wounding of a passenger or any other bodily injury suffered by a passenger, if the accident which caused the damage so sustained took place on board the aircraft or in the course of any of the operations of embarking or disembarking', for 'damage sustained in the event of the destruction or loss of, or to any registered luggage or any goods, if the occurrence which caused the damage so sustained took place during the carriage by air', or for 'damage occasioned by delay in the carriage by air of passengers, luggage or goods'. Such was the main subject matter of the Convention signed at Warsaw on 12 October 1929, which was made part of English law by means of the Carriage by Air Act, 1932. This Convention is still in force, and there are now more than seventy parties to it—far more if one counts separately all the various territories in respect of which the United Kingdom is a party. The United States also became a party to the Convention in 1934.

For the convenience of the courts, the legal profession, the airlines and the travelling public, the British Government issues from time to time Carriage by Air (Parties to Convention) Orders. Based on information received from the Polish Government, the depository of the Convention, these keep interested persons informed as to who are the parties to the Convention and in respect of what territories they are respectively parties.

The Warsaw Convention has since been amended by a Protocol concluded at The Hague on 28 September 1955, and supplemented by a Convention concluded at Guadalajara in Mexico on 18 September 1961. Powers have been taken under the Carriage by Air Act, 1961, and the Carriage by Air (Supplementary Provisions) Act, 1962, to bring these changes into force, so far as the United Kingdom is concerned, although only in the case of the Guadalajara Convention has the power been exercised. The Warsaw and Guadalajara Conventions, and the Hague Protocol, operate largely in the field of private law, and as such are outside the scope of these lectures. These are, however, of capital importance in air law, and they deserve to be mentioned here as ultimate by-products of the Paris Convention. Although the Convention was not directly concerned with private international air law, CINA had its seat in Paris, and in that city there met in 1925 upon the invitation of the French Government, the first International Conference on Private Air Law. This initiative led to the establishment of the 'Comité Internationale Technique d'Experts Juridiques Aériens' (CITEJA), the forerunner of the present Legal Committee of ICAO and the equivalent, one might say, in the air law field of the International Law Commission of the United Nations. In addition to the question of the liability of air carriers (brought to a successful conclusion at Warsaw in 1929), a number of other important matters were referred to CITEJA. They included damage caused by aircraft to property or persons on the ground; compulsory insurance; air collisions; and the legal status of the commanding officer of an aircraft. Some progress has been made with the questions originally referred to CITEJA, as well as with others, the study of which has been taken up later. But, on the whole, apart from the questions dealt with at Paris in 1919 and at Warsaw in 1929, air law has proved remarkably resistant not merely to change and growth but even to the initial elaboration of its basic rules. The reason is not far to seek. From the early preoccupation with the threat to security caused by photographically-equipped balloons down to the present desire to operate airlines as symbols of recently-won independence, aviation is a matter which Governments have never been content to leave to private initiatives or to market forces. Never, as a matter of fact, was the political aspect more to the fore than it was during the inter-war period we have just been considering. It was only too well understood that, just as the great expansion of civil aviation was made possible by the availability after the war of large numbers of surplus military aircraft, so these aircraft, and their successors, could readily be converted back to their original use. For this very reason it was to the Disarmament Conference in 1932 that the French Government submitted, in addition to a proposal to prohibit air attacks against civilians and indeed to abolish bombardment from the air altogether, a plan for the internationalization of civil air transport under a regime organized by the League of Nations. The proposal came to nothing. But we have now arrived at a stage in our lecture at which it would be convenient to look more closely at the main effort made between the two wars to clarify the law regulating aerial warfare.

The Hague Air Warfare Rules, 1923

During the Conference on the Limitation of Armament held at Washington in 1922 a resolution was passed establishing a Commission of Jurists to consider the following questions:

(a) Do existing rules of International Law adequately cover new methods of attack or defence resulting from the introduction or development, since the Hague Conference of 1907, of new agencies of warfare?

(b) If not so, what changes in the existing rules ought to be adopted in consequence thereof as a part of the law of nations?

The Washington Conference itself having dealt with submarines and gas warfare, two subjects only were referred to the Commission. These were aviation and radio. The Commission was a strong one, having Judge Bassett Moore as its chairman and including Professors de Lapradelle and Basdevant and Sir Cecil Hurst amongst its members. On aerial warfare it drew up a code of sixty-two articles. This code was never accepted by the Governments and therefore it has no claim to rank as a statement of international law apart from its own intrinsic merits and the reputation of its authors.

Admiral Rodgers, technical adviser to the United States delegation to the Commission, makes the interesting revelation, which is sufficient to explain the failure to adopt the Commission's recommendations, that the demand for a new code of rules was felt by the public rather than by the Governments. At the Hague Peace Conferences the lawyers had played a relatively minor role, the delegations consisting for the most part of diplomats, naval and military attachés, and other Service officers. The British delegation at the 1899 Conference, for instance, had no legal adviser as such, although the leader, Sir Julian Pauncefote, the British ambassador to the United States, had originally pursued a legal career. The position was admittedly rather different at the 1907 Conference, with the three leading members of the delegation, Sir Edward Fry, Sir Ernest Satow and Lord Reay, all distinguished figures in international law and with the youthful Mr. Cecil Hurst actually described as a legal adviser. In this fact alone we can perhaps discern a certain progress made by international law in the intervening period between the two conferences. Even so it would be wrong to give the impression that the Second Hague Conference was a gathering mainly of lawyers.

In 1923, however, the boot was on the other foot, and the Service officers found themselves as mere technical advisers to essentially legal delegations. As Admiral Rodgers explains, this led to a certain tension although he also assures us that 'in the end, as might be expected, the technical advisers had great weight with the heads of their respective delegations and in most points were able to convince the latter as to the correctness and applicability of their views having regard to the national policy'.

I shall now summarize the main proposals of the Commission, particularly those that are most relevant to the theme of these lectures. I shall take first the least controversial proposals.

(i) That military aircraft should bear external marks indicating their nationality and military character, and that military aircraft alone should exercise belligerent rights (Articles 1, 11 and 16).

(ii) That the use of tracer, incendiary or explosive projectiles 'by or against aircraft' should not be prohibited, even as regards those countries bound by the St. Petersburg Declaration (Article 18). This proposal to some extent sanctioned the practice of the First World War. At the same time it came dangerously near to abrogating the Declaration of St. Petersburg because, if it became generally permissible for these weapons to be used 'by or against aircraft', the continued validity of the Declaration in, for instance, land warfare would be gravely prejudiced.

(iii) That 'the use of false external marks is forbidden' (Article 19). Here the stricter rule of land warfare was preferred to the more lenient naval rule, and indeed it was specifically provided that 'except so far as special rules are here laid down and except also so far as the provisions of Chapter VII of these rules[1] or international conventions indicate that maritime law and procedure are applicable, aircraft personnel engaged in hostilities come under the laws of war and neutrality applicable to land troops in virtue of the custom and practice of international law and the various declarations and conventions to which the States concerned are parties' (Article 62).

(iv) That 'when', but only when, 'an aircraft has been disabled, the occupants when endeavouring to escape by means of a parachute must not be attacked in the course of their descent' (Article 20).

(v) That 'the use of aircraft for the purpose of disseminating propaganda shall not be treated as an illegitimate means of warfare' (Article 21). There had been some controversy on this point in the First World War. In 1917 two British officers were sentenced by the Germans to ten years' hard labour for having dropped leaflets, and in September 1918 an Austrian commander announced that 'the

[1] This Chapter deals with 'Visit and Search, Capture and Condemnation'.

dropping of manifestos and proclamations by enemy aviators constitutes a crime against the State. Any aviator who drops such manifestos, or even has them in his possession, thus puts himself outside international law, and will be considered as guilty of a crime punishable with death'. It was sometimes argued that, whereas to drop leaflets urging troops to surrender might be an act of war, to disseminate propaganda urging the civil population to revolt was not a military act at all but a political crime against the State concerned. However, in both cases mentioned, the Allies were able by threatening reprisals to stay the hands of their opponents, and in fact leaflets aimed at influencing both combatants and non-combatants were dropped on a fairly extensive scale by both sides.

(vi) That 'belligerent aircraft are bound to respect the rights of neutral Powers and to abstain within the jurisdiction of the neutral State from the commission of any act which it is the duty of that State to prevent' (Article 39).

(vii) That 'belligerent military aircraft are forbidden to enter the jurisdiction of a neutral State' (Article 40).

(viii) That 'a neutral Government must use the means at its disposal to prevent the entry within its jurisdiction of belligerent military aircraft and to compel them to alight if they have entered such jurisdiction' (Article 42).

On the question of bombardment, which was of course the core of the matter, the Commission explained that the conscience of mankind revolted against the indiscriminate launching of bombs on non-combatant populations and that the feeling was universal that limitations must be imposed. (Indeed, the study of this whole question becomes unintelligible unless it is realized that the imposition of some restriction on aerial bombardment was for public opinion in the 1920's as emotional an issue as was that of nuclear disarmament in the 1950's. It is a matter for sombre appraisal that the concern of public opinion, even though it was reflected in texts such as that put forward by the jurists in 1923, had little or no influence upon events.) The Commission realized, however, that aircraft were potent engines of war and that it was 'useless . . . to enact prohibitions unless there is an equally clear understanding of what constitutes legitimate objects of attack'. Here the Commission put little faith in the Hague Declaration of 1907 and also came to the conclusion that the test of the defended town, set out in the Hague Regulations, was of no value. Instead the Commission proposed to assert boldly that

D

'aerial bombardment for the purpose of terrorizing the civilian population, of destroying or damaging private property not of military character, or of injuring non-combatants is prohibited' (Article 22). The Commission would also go further than the 1907 rules applicable to bombardment by naval forces had gone, and would prohibit aerial bombardment not merely on account of failure to pay money contributions but even 'for the purpose of enforcing compliance with requisitions in kind' (Article 23). This, however, is a relatively minor issue.

In Article 24 the Commission faced the critical question: when is a bombardment legitimate? Here it adopted the test of a military objective, which it defined as 'an object of which the destruction or injury would constitute a distinct military advantage to the belligerent'. An attempt at clarification was made by enumerating military objectives. The list was wide and went further than the list contained in the Ninth Hague Convention of 1907. It included, as well as obvious military targets, factories engaged in the manufacture of 'distinctively military supplies' and 'lines of communication or transportation used for military purposes'. However, the Commission next proceeded to say that 'The bombardment of cities, towns, villages, dwellings or buildings not in the immediate neighbourhood of the operation of land forces is prohibited'; and that where military objectives are 'so situated, that they cannot be bombarded without the indiscriminate bombardment of the civilian population, the aircraft must abstain from bombardment'. Finally, the Commission asserted that, in the immediate neighbourhood of the operations of land forces, the bombardment of towns as such was legitimate 'provided that there exists a reasonable presumption that the military concentration is sufficiently important to justify such bombardment, having regard to the danger thus caused to the civilian population'; and in the subsequent article (Article 25) it proceeded to enjoin that, when bombardment does take place, 'all necessary steps must be taken by the commander to spare as far as possible buildings dedicated to public worship, art, science, or charitable purposes, historic monuments, hospital ships, hospitals and other places where the sick and wounded are collected, provided such buildings, objects or places are not at the time used for military purposes'.

The Hague Air Warfare Rules were not a collection of unrealistic provisions drawn up by an ignorant but well-meaning body of pacifists. They were prepared by responsible jurists guided by Service advisers. They made many concessions to the air arm, and to military necessities generally. The latitude given to bomb factories and lines of communication was wide. It is easy to see that public opinion would not have been content with anything less stringent. At the same time it is no less easy to understand why Governments could not commit themselves to the rules as they stood. The best, if not the only, defence against aerial bombardment was believed to lie in a policy of attack, or at least reprisal. To use the language of today, an air force restricted by the Hague rules would have been a less 'credible deterrent' than one free to exercise air power more widely. It is, however, to the preparations for, and the conduct of, the Second World War that we must turn in the ensuing chapter.

Chapter IV

THE SECOND WORLD WAR

As we saw in the last lecture, the experience of the First World War was inconclusive in two senses, viz.: (i) it was uncertain how valuable a weapon aerial bombardment was, or could be made to be, for the purpose of winning wars; (ii) it was uncertain what the general rules of international law were in regard to aerial bombardment, irrespective of the question whether a particular raid might or might not be justified as a reprisal. So far as Great Britain was concerned, however, there was evidence that, under pressure of bombardment from the air, public opinion tended to oscillate between demands for vengeance of the crudest kind and high-minded appeals that this country should not sink to the level of its enemies.

Despite the sincere attempt of the jurists at The Hague in 1923 to codify the laws of aerial warfare, there was very little confidence that the rules proposed by them, or any other rules, would be kept. Speaking in the House of Commons on 23 July 1923, shortly after the jurists had met, Sir Samuel Hoare, Secretary of State for Air, said: 'We see the fact that whilst air raids were sufficiently terrible even in the sporadic and infrequent form they took during the War, they would be a hundred times more terrible now. We see the fact that whilst these air raids, sporadic and infrequent as they were during the War, were none the less able to cripple the national effort and at times almost to bring the national life to a standstill, their effect would be ten times and perhaps a hundred times worse today.' In the same debate, Mr. Ramsay MacDonald, later Prime Minister, but then in Opposition, said: 'The next war will be worse than ever. There will be the blockade, and, what is more, there will be the air raids, with poison gases, which will simply devastate whole towns and whole countrysides.' Winding up the debate, the Prime Minister (Mr. Baldwin) said: 'Let us never forget that sometimes in the darkest day the beginnings of better things are not only attempted but successfully achieved. It was in the darkest days of the struggle of the Thirty Years War that Grotius worked on international law and led to the foundation of that science which, though it has not brought peace to the world, has yet brought into being a code which has helped the world in its peaceful development, and will continue to do so.' At this point, an honourable Member interjected: 'Hear, hear! He was never understood.'[1]

At the Disarmament Conference in 1932-4 various proposals were put forward for the abolition of bombing, and even of air forces; but these came to nothing.

The Royal Air Force had come into existence on 1 April 1918, as the result of the Air Force (Constitution) Act, 1917. Previously, Britain's air forces had consisted of the Royal Flying Corps (a branch of the Army) and the Royal Naval Air Service. The decision to set up an independent air force was more than just a question of Service reorganization. The nation felt deeply that in the future it would be just as dependent on air power as it had been for centuries on sea power. The new policy also committed this country earlier than others to the concept of using air power independently, a concept cherished and fought for strenuously by Marshal of the Royal Air Force Lord Trenchard, who was the first Chief of the Air Staff in 1918 and who, after a brief intermission, returned to hold that post from 1919 until 1929.

It certainly would never have been easy to accommodate within the existing laws of land and sea warfare the operations of the new air arm. But there can be no doubt that the policy of using air forces altogether independently, fostered so sedulously by Lord Trenchard, made the task of devising rules for air warfare considerably more difficult.

On 2 May 1928, Lord Trenchard submitted to his fellow Chiefs of Staff a most important memorandum. In an accompanying letter he referred to a controversy which had arisen because his colleagues in the other Services did not appear to accept 'the contention of the Air Staff that in future wars air attacks would most certainly be carried out against most vital centres of communication and munition centres, no matter where they were situated'. Whereas the other Service Manuals stated that the object of the Navy (or the Army) was to destroy the enemy's navy (or army), the object of the Air Force would not merely be to destroy the opposing air forces but to 'break down the enemy's means of resistance by attacks on objectives selected as most likely to achieve this end'. Asking himself the question whether this doctrine violated any true principle of war, or would be contrary either to international law or to the dictates of humanity, Lord Trenchard came to a negative answer. He cited the fact that the jurists of 1923 had allowed attacks on military objectives

[1] *Parliamentary Debates, Commons* (1923), Vol. 167, Cols. 82, 120 and 178.

and he relied also on the naval practice, sanctioned by the Ninth Hague Convention of 1907, of bombarding military objectives in undefended towns. If such attacks were not allowed, 'a belligerent would be able to secure complete immunity for his war manufactures and depots merely by locating them in a large city, which would, in effect, become *neutral* territory—a position which the opposing belligerent would never accept. What is illegitimate, as being contrary to the dictates of humanity, is the indiscriminate bombing of a city for the sole purpose of terrorizing the civilian population. It is an entirely different matter to terrorize munition workers (men and women) into absenting themselves from work or stevedores into abandoning the loading of a ship with munitions through fear of an air attack upon the factory or dock concerned.' In any case, concluded Lord Trenchard, 'there is not the slightest doubt that in the next war both sides will send their aircraft out without scruple to bomb those objectives which they consider the most suitable'.

Such were the views on aerial warfare held at the Air Ministry between the wars and whatever may be thought of them, it is clear, and of course not surprising, that that Ministry had given more thought to the implications of independent air operations than had the other Service ministries. There is something rather unconvincing about the attempts of the Admiralty and the War Office to invoke international law as a justification for ruling out of order a means of warfare which they disliked for other reasons, chief among which was perhaps the consideration that it would result in the Royal Air Force obtaining a larger share of the limited credits available for defence purposes. This does not mean, however, that there was no force in their legal arguments.

Sir G. F. Milne, Chief of the Imperial General Staff, pointed out with some cogency that 'if it is held to be justifiable to bomb undefended towns by aircraft, it should equally be held justifiable to sink merchant ships, and to bombard undefended ports or towns, whether from the sea or from the land'. As regards the ethical aspects of the Air Force proposals it would be for His Majesty's Government 'to accept or to refuse a doctrine which, put into plain English, amounts to one which advocates unrestricted warfare against the civil population of one's enemy'.

Sir C. Madden, Chief of the Naval Staff, evinced considerable scepticism as to the claims made by the Air Force and feared that 'there will be dispersion on bombing operations which will have little military effect on the conduct of the war and which will bear no relation to the operations on land of the Army or on sea of the Navy'. Turning to international law, he said that the operations envisaged by the Royal Air Force would endanger civilian life 'to a far greater degree than has ever hitherto been contemplated under International Law'. He added the following observation: 'As a sea nation we oppose unrestricted submarine warfare, and, whilst admitting the right of visit and search and the sinking on occasion, of enemy merchant ships, maintain that under international law full arrangements must be made for the safety of non-combatants. If we now advocate as an object of the Air Force a policy of air bombing, in which proper provision cannot be made for the safety of non-combatants, we are hardly in a position to meet the arguments which will be put forward by a continental military Power in favour of unrestricted submarine war at sea against merchant vessels.'[1]

Despite the bravado of its air chiefs, the British Government showed considerable circumspection in the matter of air raids when war actually broke out on 3 September 1939. Two days earlier President Roosevelt had addressed an appeal to the four Governments of the principal European nations likely to be engaged in war to declare that they would 'in no event and under no circumstances undertake bombardment from the air of civilian populations or unfortified cities, upon the understanding that the same rules of warfare shall be scrupulously observed by all their opponents'. The next day the British and French Governments confirmed that they would not bomb from the air 'any except strictly military objectives in the narrowest sense of the word'. At first this policy was strictly carried out and Sir William Malkin, Legal Adviser to the Foreign Office, was consulted as to whether it would be legitimate to attack even so obvious a military objective as the Kiel Canal.[2] Not until 15 May 1940 was Bomber Command authorized to attack east of the Rhine, and even then Sir Charles Portal, Air Officer Commanding-in-Chief, Bomber Command, was told to concentrate on oil installations and aircraft factories. He was further told that 'in no circumstances should night bombing be allowed to degenerate into mere indiscriminate action, which is contrary to the policy of His Majesty's Government'.[3]

[1] Sir Charles Webster and Noble Frankland, *The Strategic Air Offensive against Germany 1939–1945* (1961), Vol. IV, Appendix 2.
[2] Webster and Frankland, op. cit., Vol. I, p. 105.
[3] Directive of Air Vice-Marshal W. S. Douglas (Deputy Chief of the Air Staff) to Air Marshal C. F. A. Portal (Air Officer Commanding-in-Chief, Bomber Command), 4 June 1940, op. cit., Vol. IV, p. 112.

Under the impact of German raids on English cities, there was, as the official historians, Sir Charles Webster and Mr. Noble Frankland, tell us, an 'increasing insistence of the Prime Minister and of members of his government on a more ruthless bombing policy'. Consequently, on 13 December 1940, the War Cabinet approved a plan for an attack on Mannheim, the object of which, as Sir Richard Peirse, then Air Officer Commanding-in-Chief, Bomber Command, explained, was 'to concentrate the maximum amount of damage in the centre of the town'. The attack, which was carried out three nights later, seems, however, not to have heralded any immediate change of policy but rather to have been executed as a retaliation for raids on Coventry and Southampton.[1]

In a report drawn up on 7 January 1941, the Chiefs of Staff included 'morale' as one of seven possible targets on which to concentrate aerial bombardment, the others being 'the German air force, anti-invasion targets, transportation, industries, naval objectives and oil'. It was recommended that Bomber Command concentrate on oil, with industries, transportation and 'morale' as convenient secondary targets. However, it was said: 'Morale as a main target is one which it may prove profitable to turn to as a long-term objective for our expanded bomber force, and when the state of German morale is less robust than it is at the moment.'[2]

Notwithstanding this report, the policy still was to concentrate on oil targets. Thus, on 15 January 1941, Air Chief Marshal Sir Wilfred Freeman (Vice-Chief of the Air Staff), writing to Air Marshal Sir Richard Peirse (Air Officer Commanding-in-Chief, Bomber Command), said: 'It has been decided that the sole primary aim of your bomber offensive, until further orders, should be the destruction of the German synthetic oil plants.' Secondary targets were to be 'the enemy's main industrial towns and communications'.[3]

However, a directive of 9 July 1941, from Air Vice-Marshal N. H. Bottomley (Deputy Chief of the Air Staff) to Air Marshal Sir Richard Peirse (Air Officer Commanding-in-Chief, Bomber Command), stated as follows:

I am directed to inform you that a comprehensive review of the enemy's present political, economic and military situation discloses that the weakest points in his armour lie in the morale of the civil population and in his inland transportation system. . . .
I am to request that you will direct the main effort of the bomber force,

---

[1] Op. cit., Vol. I, pp. 162–3, 226.
[2] Op. cit., Vol. IV, p. 188.   [3] Op. cit., Vol. IV, p. 132.

until further instructions, towards dislocating the German transportation system and to destroying the morale of the civilian population as a whole and of the industrial workers in particular.[1]

A slight but subtle change of emphasis is to be detected in the directive of 14 February 1942, from Air Vice-Marshal N. H. Bottomley (Deputy Chief of the Air Staff) to Air Marshal J. E. A. Baldwin (Acting Air Officer Commanding-in-Chief, Bomber Command). This said:

A review has been made of the directions given to you in Air Ministry letter dated 9.7.41, and it has been decided that the primary object of your operations should now be focussed on the morale of the enemy civil population and, in particular, of the industrial workers.[2]

All the directives we have so far considered were thus issued before Sir Arthur Harris became Air Officer Commanding-in-Chief, Bomber Command. He took up this post on 22 February 1942.

Finally, on 21 January 1943, the famous 'Casablanca Directive' was issued by the Combined Chiefs of Staff to 'the appropriate British and United States Air Force Commanders to govern the operation of the British and United States Bomber Commands in the United Kingdom'. It was forwarded by Air Vice-Marshal Bottomley to Sir Arthur Harris on 4 February 1943, in replacement of the general directive of 14 February 1942. It said: 'Your primary object will be the progressive destruction and dislocation of the German military, industrial and economic system, and the undermining of the morale of the German people to a point where their capacity for armed resistance is fatally weakened.'[3]

Now let us consider the execution of this policy. In a series of raids on Hamburg in July and August 1943, nearly 8000 tons of bombs were dropped, about half of them incendiaries. Approximately 50,000 people were killed, most of them as a result of asphyxiation resulting from the creation of a fire-storm. The raids on Dresden in February 1945 were estimated to have caused 135,000 deaths, as against a total of about 70,000 killed when the first atomic bomb was dropped on Hiroshima a few months later. The phenomenal damage at Dresden was also largely due to a fire-storm, brought about by the dropping of thousands of incendiary bombs, most of which weighed only a few pounds each.

[1] Op. cit., Vol. IV, p. 135. [2] Op. cit., Vol. IV, p. 143.
[3] Op. cit., Vol. IV, p. 153.

Although there was much elation in Great Britain at the growing hitting power of Bomber Command, there was also some concern, as the following incidents show. On 6 May 1942, Sir Archibald Sinclair, Secretary of State for Air, was asked by Mr. J. McGovern whether, for the raids on Lübeck and Rostock, instructions had been given to the Royal Air Force to destroy workmen's dwellings. He replied that the objects of the bombing offensive were to destroy the capacity of Germany to make war. 'No instruction has been given', he said, 'to destroy dwelling houses rather than armament factories, but it is impossible to distinguish in night bombing between the factories and the dwellings which surround them.'[1]

On 31 March 1943, the Secretary of State was asked by Mr. R. R. Stokes whether instructions had been given to British airmen to engage in area bombing rather than limit their attention to purely military targets. He replied: 'The targets of Bomber Command are always military, but night bombing of military objectives necessarily involves bombing the area in which they are situated.'[2] A more protracted exchange along similar lines took place between Mr. Stokes and Sir Archibald Sinclair on 1 December 1943.[3]

The official history contains the following revealing passage:

He [Sir Archibald Sinclair] usually, and, on public occasions, invariably, suggested that Bomber Command was aiming at military or industrial installations, as, of course, it sometimes was. He did not conceal that severe and sometimes vast damage was done to residential areas, but he either implied, or on some occasions said, that all this was incidental and even regrettable. Only in this way, he explained to Sir Charles Portal (then Chief of the Air Staff) in October 1943, could he satisfy the enquiries of the Archbishop of Canterbury, the Moderator of the Church of Scotland and other significant religious leaders whose moral condemnation of the bombing offensive might, he observed, disturb the morale of Bomber Command crews. This latter consideration was, the Secretary of State thought, more important than another which Sir Arthur Harris had raised, namely, that the Bomber Command crews might form the impression that they were being asked to perform deeds which the Air Ministry was ashamed to admit.[4]

On 9 February 1944, the matter was debated in the House of Lords. After the Bishop of Chichester and Lord Lang of Lambeth had made eloquent speeches, urging restraint, Viscount Cranborne, Secretary

[1] *Parliamentary Debates, Commons* (1941–42), Vol. 379, Col. 1364.
[2] *Parliamentary Debates, Commons* (1942–43), Vol. 388, Col. 155.
[3] *Parliamentary Debates, Commons* (1943–44), Vol. 395, Cols. 337–8.
[4] Webster and Frankland, op. cit., Vol. III, p. 116.

of State for Dominion Affairs, replying for the Government, said:

Your Lordships will remember that we have never concentrated upon sleepy country towns and villages. That would not only have been unnecessarily brutal; it would have been utterly futile from our point of view. But I would emphasize this to the right reverend Prelate: the great centres of administration, of production and of communication are themselves military targets in a total war. You cannot escape that fact . . . these great German war industries can only be paralysed by bringing the whole life of the cities in which they are situated to a standstill, making it quite impossible for the workmen to carry on their work. That is a fact we may have to face and I do face it. It is, I suggest, a full justification for the present bombing campaign. I am sure that your Lordships would not refuse to accept the idea of shelling cities and towns in the front line. Nobody likes it but it has to be done for the purpose of winning wars. The German cities which I have mentioned are in the front line and they must be bombarded.[1]

The controversy became most fierce after the Dresden raids. On 6 March 1945, Mr. Stokes read out in the House of Commons an Associated Press despatch which, he claimed, had been released by the censor in Great Britain at 7.30 p.m. on 17 February, but suppressed four hours later. The despatch, based on a misunderstanding of a statement made by an Air Commodore at a press conference at Supreme Headquarters, Allied Expeditionary Force, contained the following sentence: 'Allied Air Chiefs have made the long-awaited decision to adopt deliberate terror-bombings of German populated centres as a ruthless expedient to hasten Hitler's doom.' Mr. Stokes also said in his speech: 'Leaving aside strategic bombing, which I question very much, and tactical bombing, with which I agree, if it is done with a reasonable measure of accuracy, there is no case whatever under any conditions, in my view, for terror bombing.' Replying for the Government, the Under-Secretary of State for Air, Commander Brabner, said: 'We are not wasting our bombers on purely terror tactics. Our job is to destroy the enemy. . . . We are concentrating on war targets.'[2]

The resulting furore led to Sir Winston Churchill writing on 28 March what the official historians describe as 'among the least felicitous of the Prime Minister's long series of war-time minutes'. It reads as follows:

It seems to me that the moment has come when the question of bombing of German cities simply for the sake of increasing the terror, though under

---

[1] *Parliamentary Debates, Lords* (1943–44), Vol. 130, Cols. 737–55.
[2] *Parliamentary Debates, Commons* (1944–45), Vol. 408, Cols. 1900–1, 1989–90.

other pretexts, should be reviewed. Otherwise we shall come into control of an utterly ruined land. We shall not, for instance, be able to get housing materials out of Germany for our own needs because some temporary provision would have to be made for the Germans themselves. The destruction of Dresden remains a serious query against the conduct of Allied bombing. I am of the opinion that military objectives must henceforward be more strictly studied in our own interests rather than that of the enemy.

The Foreign Secretary has spoken to me on this subject, and I feel the need for more precise concentration upon military objectives, such as oil and communications behind the immediate battle-zone, rather than on mere acts of terror and wanton destruction, however impressive.[1]

David Irving comments:

This was indeed a remarkable document. Two possible interpretations were placed upon it by those who learned of its contents: either the minute was hastily penned in the heat and turmoil of great events, and at a time when the Prime Minister was under considerable personal strain, simply recording the lessons learned from the aftermath of Dresden; or it could be construed as a carefully-phrased attempt at burdening for posterity the responsibility for the Dresden raids on to his Chiefs of Staff, and, perhaps more appositely, on to Bomber Command and Sir Arthur Harris.

Irving concludes, however, that 'it seems more charitable to accept the first alternative outlined above than the second'.[2] Sir Winston was in fact persuaded to amend his minute, so that it read as follows:

It seems to me that the moment has come when the question of the so-called 'area bombing' of German cities should be reviewed from the point of view of our own interests. If we come into control of an entirely ruined land, there will be a great shortage of accommodation for ourselves and our Allies and we shall be unable to get housing materials out of Germany for our own needs because some temporary provision would have to be made for the Germans themselves. We must see to it that our attacks do not do more harm to ourselves in the long run than they do to the enemy's immediate war effort. . . .[3]

In this form, both references to bombing for the sake of terror having been removed, the minute proved acceptable to the Air Staff. Nevertheless, the suspicion remained that the Government—including Mr. Attlee's subsequent Labour Administration as well as Sir Winston's war-time one—were anxious in some way to disown Sir Arthur Harris, who was not allowed to issue a Despatch and who did not receive a peerage like the other Service chiefs of comparable

[1] Webster and Frankland, op. cit., Vol. III, p. 112.
[2] *The Destruction of Dresden* (1963), p. 229.
[3] Webster and Frankland, op. cit., Vol. III, p. 117.

rank. As the official historians put it, 'The Prime Minister and others in authority seemed to turn away from the subject as though it were distasteful to them and as though they had forgotten their own recent efforts to initiate and maintain the offensive.'[1]

For their part, Webster and Frankland, in addition to praising the leadership of Sir Arthur Harris, unhesitatingly acquit him of any charge of conducting war improperly. They say:

These moral issues are likely to continue to be long debated, and the verdicts will doubtless to some extent be conditioned by the circumstances of the ages in which they are reached. It should now, nevertheless, be clear that neither the Air Staff nor Sir Arthur Harris can justly be accused of waging war in a different moral sense from that approved by the Government. Moreover, it should equally be clear that at no stage of the war was the area bombing offensive wanton. On the contrary, it was a carefully designed strategic plan intended to contribute to the most rapid and the most economical defeat of Germany. Though the area offensive, even in the light of the various operational circumstances, is open to many strategic criticisms, it is difficult to see why it should bear unfavourable moral comparison with naval blockade or some other kinds of warfare.[2]

Moreover, Sir Arthur Harris is quite capable of defending himself. After pointing out that deaths from Allied bombing in Germany probably amounted to 305,000, as against 800,000 caused by the blockade in the First World War, he goes on in his book to say:

Whenever the fact that our aircraft occasionally killed women and children is cast in my teeth I always produce this example of the blockade, although there are endless others to be got from wars of the past. I never forget, as so many do, that in all normal warfare of the past, and of the not distant past, it was the common practice to besiege cities and, if they refused to surrender when called upon with due formality to do so, every living thing in them was in the end put to the sword. Even in the more civilized times of today the siege of cities, accompanied by the bombardment of the city as a whole, is still a normal practice; in no circumstances were women and children allowed to pass out of the city, because their presence in it and their consumption of food would inevitably hasten the end of the siege. And as to bombardment, what city in what war has ever failed to receive the maximum bombardment from all enemy artillery within range so long as it has continued resistance? International law can always be argued pro. and con., but in this matter of the use of aircraft in war there is, it so happens, no international law at all.[3]

The view that there were no rules of international law applicable to aerial warfare is likewise shared by the official historians and by

---

[1] Op. cit., Vol. III, p. 284.   [2] Op. cit., Vol. III, pp. 116–17.
[3] *Bomber Offensive* (1947), pp. 176–7.

David Irving. Is this view correct? It is suggested that all these authors are in error because they seem unable to envisage any rules of international law other than those contained in treaties. For them it is sufficient to point out the failure of the Governments to ratify the rules proposed by the jurists in 1923, although even on that view the provisions of the Hague Regulations (1907) should not have been ignored. For these authors the rules of customary international law and 'the general principles of law recognized by civilized nations' do not seem to exist. They appear unaware that the international legal system always has consisted, and still consists, mainly of customary rules. These authors seem unaware too that, by virtue of what they authorized and what they did in the Second World War, the statesmen and the air chiefs whose exploits they were describing were actually helping to fashion rules of aerial warfare. Even if this involved the violation of existing rules—on this point I express no opinion at this stage—again that would not be exceptional. International law is frequently made and remade in that way. As an example one could quote the fate of the three-mile limit for territorial waters, once a nearly universal rule but recently dishonoured so much that its continued existence as a rule is open to question, at any rate in time of peace.

I referred in the last lecture to the 'rude practice of war' as being a source which should be examined for the purpose of arriving at the rules of war. This does not involve giving a blank cheque to the doctrine of military necessity. What it does mean, though, is seeking the laws of war, just like other rules of international law, through the practice of States rather than through the speculation of writers. That, at any rate, is the reason why I have examined in this lecture the instructions given to the bomber chiefs and the statements of their political superiors in justification, or attempted justification, of those instructions.

On this basis, then, can we deduce the rules of aerial bombardment as they emerged from the Second World War? For reasons of space, it will be necessary to leave the atomic bomb out of this discussion. The legality of nuclear warfare turns on a number of altogether separate issues which cannot be gone into here. These include, *inter alia*, (i) the provisions of the Hague Regulations (1907) relating to the use of poison and poisoned weapons; (ii) the Geneva Protocol of 17 June 1925, which prohibits the use in war of 'asphyxiating, poisonous or other gases, and of all analogous liquids, materials or devices'; and (iii) more recent instruments such as the Genocide Convention of 1948, and a resolution adopted by the General Assembly on 24 November 1961, in which that body declared that 'the use of nuclear and thermonuclear weapons is contrary to the spirit, letter and aims of the United Nations and, as such, a direct violation of the United Nations Charter'.[1]

Summing up the lessons to be drawn from the Second World War itself, the significant failure of the International Military Tribunal at Nuremberg in 1946 to deal with the question of aerial bombardments, and the provisions of post-war agreements, such as the Geneva Conventions of 1949 and the Hague Convention on the Protection of Cultural Property in the Event of Armed Conflict, 1954, a leading authority on the laws of war, Professor Schwarzenberger, concluded that under modern conditions the standard of civilization has retreated before the necessities of war; that the traditional distinction between combatants and non-combatants has largely disappeared; and that the only persons who may still expect immunity from acts of warfare are persons who are *both* unconnected with military operations or the production of war materials *and* reside in areas that are 'sufficiently remote' from likely target areas. As for these target areas the onus is now not so much on the attacker to show that he has attacked a 'defended place' or a 'military objective' as upon the parties to a conflict to establish, preferably by agreement, 'hospital and safety zones and localities so organized as to protect from the effects of war, wounded, sick and aged persons, children under fifteen, expectant mothers and mothers of children under seven', and also 'neutralized zones intended to shelter from the effects of war the following persons without distinction: (*a*) wounded and sick combatants or non-combatants; (*b*) civilian persons who take no part in hostilities, and who, while they reside in the zones, perform no work of a military character'.[2]

---

[1] See G. Schwarzenberger, *The Legality of Nuclear Weapons* (1958).

[2] G. Schwarzenberger, 'Report on Self-Defence under the Charter of the United Nations and the Use of Prohibited Weapons' in *International Law Association. Report of the Fiftieth Conference, Brussels* (1962). See also articles 14 and 15 of the Geneva Convention relative to the Protection of Civilian Persons in Time of War, 12 August 1949, from which these citations are taken.
An even more revealing example of the limited nature of the concessions which military necessity is now prepared to make to the standard of civilization is provided by Article 8(1) of the Convention for the Protection of Cultural Property in the Event of Armed Conflict, adopted at The Hague on 14 May 1954. This reads as follows: 'There may be placed under special protection a limited number of refuges intended to shelter movable cultural property in the event of armed conflict, of centres containing monuments and other immovable cultural property of very great importance, provided that they: (*a*) are situated at an adequate

This is of course a desperate solution, abandoning as it does any attempt to distinguish in a general way between combatants and non-combatants. Nevertheless, the policy of endeavouring to protect certain classes of persons against the horrors of war by herding them into sanctuaries has the merit of probably being the only realistic solution under modern conditions; and there is no merit in the laws of war if they do not accord with realities. Moreover, this solution was tried, and worked well, in the Sino–Japanese war in 1937–8.[1]

Professor Schwarzenberger concluded his report as follows:

In view of the conduct of air warfare during the Second World War, the inconclusiveness in this respect of relevant post-1945 treaties and the generally known preparations made by all major Powers for air and missile warfare, it appears impossible to state with any confidence that near-total air and missile warfare runs counter to the contemporary laws and customs of war.[2]

Not so very different was the view expressed by Sir Hersch Lauterpacht in an article which, if not among the best known of his writings, is certainly one of the most profound. Firm upholder of the authority of international law though he was, this great scholar and judge conceded that those who maintain that aerial bombardment as generally carried on in the Second World War violated international law 'must undertake the exacting task of proving that absolute respect for the life of the enemy civilian is a rule so fundamental, so overriding, and so uncontroversial as to render immune from direct military attack objects and localities whose destruction the belligerent considers vital for his purpose'.[3] In the light of the rules which permitted the bombardment of defended towns in land warfare—and it should never be forgotten that the German-controlled air space was very heavily defended by a combination of radar, fighter aeroplanes and anti-aircraft guns—and even of undefended towns in naval war, Sir Hersch Lauterpacht did not think that this burden of proof could be discharged. He stressed, however, that in the rule which clearly forbids terrorization of the civilian population

---

distance from any large industrial centre or from any important military objective constituting a vulnerable point, such as, for example, an aerodrome, broadcasting station, establishment engaged upon work of national defence, a port or railway station of relative importance or a main line of communication; (b) are not used for military purposes.'
[1] J. M. Spaight, *Air Power and War Rights* (3rd ed. 1947), p. 256.
[2] Loc. cit., p. 218.
[3] *British Year Book of International Law*, 29 (1952), p. 365.

as an avowed object of attack not incidental to lawful operations 'lies the last vestige of the claim that war can be legally regulated at all'.[1]

Having weighed all the evidence, and conscious as I am of the importance of the issue, I find myself compelled to come to the same conclusion. Put into plain English, this means—if we may employ the same terms as Mr. Stokes used in his intervention in the House of Commons in 1945—that modern international law permits 'strategic' and, of course, 'tactical' bombing in time of war, but forbids 'terror-bombing'.[2]

[1] Ibid., p. 369.

[2] No attempt is made in these lectures to consider the lawfulness of the recourse to force by States. There is a vast literature on this question. See, especially, D. W. Bowett, *Self-defence in International Law* (1958), Manchester University Press, and I. Brownlie, *International Law and the Use of Force by States* (1963), Oxford at the Clarendon Press. The present writer is of the view that, even if force is resorted to illegally, the interests of humanity are best served by endeavouring to ensure the application of the laws of war. The strict argument that, since international law now generally forbids recourse to force, an aggressor has no 'belligerent rights', would soon lead in practice to a situation in which the aggressor acknowledged no duties either, and thus the hostilities would degenerate into completely unregulated violence. No more palatable is the theory that, since the forces suppressing an aggressor (e.g. United Nations Forces) are acting on behalf of the international community rather than engaging in war in the sense of a contestation between States, they need not abide by the laws of war. The application of this theory too would lead to completely unregulated violence. On this question see Chapter 15 of D. W. Bowett, *United Nations Forces* (1964), London, Stevens.

Chapter V

SOME CONTEMPORARY PROBLEMS
IN INTERNATIONAL AIR LAW

CIVIL AVIATION UNDER THE CHICAGO CONVENTION, 1944

EVEN before hostilities ended, President Roosevelt realized the necessity of providing a sound basis for the organization of civil aviation after the war. He therefore invited a large number of Governments to attend a conference in Chicago. Fifty-two Governments attended.

Implicit in this step was the recognition that it would no longer do to organize civil aviation on a partial or regional footing. Owing to the increased range of aircraft nothing less than a world-wide arrangement would now suffice.

The most important achievement of the Conference was the formulation of the Convention on International Civil Aviation, which I shall refer to simply as 'the Chicago Convention'. This Convention (Part II of which is the Constitution of the International Civil Aviation Organization—ICAO) came into force on 4 April 1947. It will be considered presently. In the intervening period there was in existence the Provisional International Civil Aviation Organization (PICAO), which was established on 6 June 1945, and which operated under an Interim Agreement on International Civil Aviation also concluded at the Chicago Conference.

As well as the main Convention and the Interim Agreement, the Chicago Conference drew up two other agreements. These were the International Air Services Transit Agreement (known as the 'Two-Freedoms' Agreement) and the International Air Transport Agreement (known as the 'Five-Freedoms' Agreement). The Conference also adopted a number of resolutions. In one of these it resolved that certain studies on technical matters of the kind dealt with in the annexes in the Paris Convention, which had been carried on at Chicago but not completed, be accepted as models for the annexes to the new Chicago Convention. In another, the Conference, recognizing the part that bilateral agreements would have to play in

58

developing international civil aviation, prepared a 'Form of Standard Agreement for Provisional Air Routes'. It was recommended that the States parties to such agreements set out in an annex thereto 'a description of the routes and of the rights granted whether of transit only, of non-traffic stops or of commercial entry as the case may be, and the conditions incidental to the granting of the rights'; and that the agreements themselves provide for such matters as equality of treatment in airport charges and the right to bring in fuel, lubricating oil and spare parts. Further, the agreements should provide for exemption from customs duties of 'the fuel, lubricating oils, spare parts, regular equipment and aircraft stores retained on board civil aircraft of the airlines of the contracting parties authorized to operate the routes and services described in the annex', and should allow contracting parties to revoke a permit granted to an airline or another State in cases where such parties are not satisfied that 'substantial ownership and effective control' of the airline in question are vested in nationals of a party to the agreement, or in case of failure of an airline to comply with the laws of the State over which it operates or to perform its obligations under the agreement.

It remains therefore to consider in a summary way the provisions of the main Convention[1] and of the 'Two-Freedoms' and 'Five-Freedoms' Agreements.

The Convention has three main Parts. Part I deals with 'Air Navigation'. Part II, as already stated, is the Constitution of ICAO. Part III deals with 'International Air Transport'. Although there is no rigid dividing line, and although both raise issues of great legal importance, it may be said that, in general, 'air navigation' refers to the technical and operational aspects of civil aviation, and 'air transport' to the commercial and economic aspects. In the Preamble the parties to the Convention mention their desire 'that international civil aviation may be developed in a safe and orderly manner and that international air transport services may be established on the basis of equality of opportunity and operated soundly and economically'. As was true of the Paris Convention for the Regulation of Aerial Navigation, 1919, and as has also been shown to be true of the Convention for the Establishment of the Inter-governmental Maritime Consultative Organization concluded at Geneva in 1948, it has proved much easier to deal satisfactorily with the technical aspects of a means of international transport than with the economic aspects.

---

[1] The summary given here will be very brief, since the text of the Convention, as amended, is printed in Appendix II.

Confirming the principle laid down in 1919, and long since strengthened by uniform State practice, Article 1 provides that 'the contracting States recognize that every State has complete and exclusive sovereignty over the air space above its territory'. Now that space flight has become possible, considerable speculation has arisen as to precisely what Article 1 means. There are various schools of thought. According to one school, both the Paris and the Chicago Conventions had it in mind only to deal with the activities of aircraft depending for their flight on aerodynamic lift. Therefore, this school says, air space should be interpreted accordingly, and the maximum height up to which States should be permitted to exercise sovereignty would be of the order of 20–25 miles. According to another school, 'air space' must be given its literal meaning, and the scientists must be asked to pronounce at what height 'air' ends. This they are loath to do with the degree of precision required by lawyers, and, on this view, the upper limit of the air space might be placed anywhere between 500 miles and 10,000 miles above the surface of the earth. All sorts of other limits could be, indeed have been, suggested. So far as the British Government are concerned, their view was stated by Viscount Hailsham (as he then was) in the House of Lords on 11 June 1959, as follows:

Her Majesty's Government consider that sovereignty over space above national territory cannot extend indefinitely upwards. It cannot, however, be said that international law has yet determined the exact limit to be placed on the extension of sovereignty upwards or what legal regime should apply in realms of outer space to which sovereignty does not extend. There are still too many unsolved problems in this field to justify the adoption of any sweeping legal propositions, in whatever direction they tend.[1]

Other Governments have been similarly coy, and so has the United Nations as a whole. On 14 July 1959, the *Ad Hoc* Committee on the Peaceful Use of Outer Space, established by the General Assembly, stated that 'it was generally believed that the determination of precise limits for air space and outer space did not present a legal problem calling for priority consideration at this moment'. The Committee also noted that 'the solution of the problems which it had identified as susceptible of priority treatment was not dependent upon the establishment of such limits'.[2] Since then, although the General Assembly has adopted a number of useful resolutions on outer space,

[1] *Parliamentary Debates, Lords* (1958–59), Vol. 216, Col. 975.
[2] U.N. doc. A/4141, p. 68, paragraph 28.

and although a tendency is clearly developing for outer space to be governed by a legal regime distinct from that which regulates air space, no progress has been made towards prescribing a definite boundary between the two zones. Nor is it certain that a boundary ever will be fixed, or even that the ultimate solution will be in terms of two zones only. A practical solution would seem to be to fix the limit of the air space so that it is just below the height maintained by space vehicles in orbit. This, however, would still pose a problem for small States who, in order to get their satellites into orbit, would require transit rights through the air space of their neighbours. In turn, this problem might be solved by creating an intermediate zone between national air space and outer space. Such a zone would, like the air space, be part of the territory of the subjacent State, but a right of innocent passage would exist through it on the analogy of the similar right enjoyed by ships through territorial waters. Sensible as these solutions may seem, however, it cannot be pretended that there is any authority for them in the Chicago Convention. They will have to be arrived at, if at all, either by a new convention or by a development of customary law on the basis of State practice. At least there is nothing in the Chicago Convention which would prevent such solutions being reached, if they proved to be sound.

These lectures, however, are not about space law, and so we must come down again, if not quite to earth, at least to the heights at which the normal military and civil aircraft of today fly.

Article 2 of the Chicago Convention confirms that national air space includes the air space above territorial waters as well as above land areas. This is an important factor, which weighed considerably with many States represented at the two United Nations Conferences on the Law of the Sea, held at Geneva in 1958 and 1960. These States feared that, if territorial waters were extended, their aviation would be affected as well as their maritime interests—in fact more so, because, whereas under customary international law foreign shipping enjoys the right of innocent passage through territorial waters, there is no corresponding right for aircraft to fly through the air space of other States. Such rights as aircraft do enjoy have to be granted either in a multilateral convention, such as that of Chicago, or in bilateral agreements.

Article 3 provides that the Convention applies only to civil aircraft, and not to State aircraft, i.e. 'aircraft used in military, customs and police services'. However, as with the Paris Convention, the important principle is preserved that an aircraft is not a 'State

61

aircraft' in this sense merely because it is owned by a State or by a State-subsidized airline.

Article 5 of the Convention, entitled 'Right of non-scheduled flight' is extremely important for the reason that, complicated though it is, it grants such rights of flight as are available under the Convention. It may help to understand Article 5 if we first recite Article 6, which reads as follows: 'No scheduled international air service may be operated over or into the territory of a contracting State, except with the special permission or other authorization of that State, and in accordance with the terms of such permission or authorization'. Harshly restrictive though this article is, it is tolerably clear. The draftsmen were determined to avoid the ambiguities that arose in regard to Article 15 of the Paris Convention during the period between 1919 and 1929. The only question that needs to be considered is precisely what constitutes a 'scheduled international air service'. From Article 96 of the Convention it is possible to deduce that an international air service is a service which passes through the air space over the territory of more than one State and which is performed by aircraft for the public transport of passengers, mail or cargo. The Council of ICAO completed the definition in 1952 when it said that in addition the service must be performed 'for remuneration, in such a manner that each flight is open to use by members of the public' and that it must be 'operated, so as to serve traffic between the same two or more points, either (i) according to a published timetable, or (ii) with flights so regular or frequent that they constitute a recognizably systematic series'.

If a service is a 'scheduled international air service', it is fairly and squarely caught by the provisions of Article 6.[1] If, however, an aircraft is not engaged in a 'scheduled international air service', the possibilities open to it are more interesting. At this point we must return to Article 5, which reads as follows:

Each contracting State agrees that all aircraft of the other contracting States, being aircraft not engaged in scheduled international air services, shall have the right, subject to the observance of the terms of this Convention, to make flights into or in transit non-stop across its territory and to make stops for non-traffic purposes without the necessity of obtaining

---

[1] It is also caught by Article 68 which says that 'Each contracting State may, subject to the provisions of this Convention, designate the route to be followed within its territory by any international air service and the airports which any such service may use'. Curiously enough, Article 96(a) defines an 'air service' as 'any *scheduled* air service performed by aircraft for the public transport of passengers, mail or cargo'.

prior permission, and subject to the right of the State flown over to require landing. Each contracting State nevertheless reserves the right, for reasons of safety of flight, to require aircraft desiring to proceed over regions which are inaccessible or without adequate air navigation facilities to follow prescribed routes, or to obtain special permission for such flights.

Such aircraft, if engaged in the carriage of passengers, cargo or mail for remuneration or hire on other than scheduled international air services, shall also, subject to the provisions of Article 7,[1] have the privilege of taking on or discharging passengers, cargo, or mail, subject to the right of any State where such embarkation or discharge takes place to impose such regulations, conditions or limitations as it may consider desirable.

The meaning of this provision has been much disputed. There is little doubt that it gives reasonably extensive rights of flight to purely private aircraft, and this appears to be the principal reason why the Soviet Union, which was not represented at Chicago, has refused subsequently to adhere to the Convention. But the scope for private flying in international aviation is not great, and the real controversy turns on the question whether companies who operate 'charter' or 'taxi' services for remuneration, but on a non-scheduled basis, are or are not required to obtain the permission of the States into which they fly. When the Convention was drawn up, it does not seem to have been thought that these activities would be of much importance. However, these activities have developed, and would clearly have developed a great deal more if an interpretation had been put on Article 5 enabling them to take place without the necessity of obtaining the permission of Governments. There would then have been a very strong temptation to take advantage of the loophole and to disguise as 'non-scheduled' services which were in reality 'scheduled'.

That this has not happened is due to the fact that, although the ICAO Secretariat at one time favoured giving Article 5 a liberal interpretation, Governments as a whole have not done so and have been supported in their attitude by the ICAO Council. Some progress towards liberalization, however, has been made, notably by the Multi-lateral Agreement on Commercial Rights of Non-Scheduled Air Services in Europe, which was concluded among a number of European countries on 30 April 1956, and came into force on 21 August 1957.

The United Kingdom became a party on 11 January 1960. In the Preamble to this Agreement the parties state that it is their policy 'that aircraft engaged in non-scheduled commercial flights within Europe which do not harm their scheduled services may be freely

[1] Article 7 reserves the 'cabotage' right for the subjacent State exclusively.

admitted to their territories for the purpose of taking on or discharging traffic'. The Agreement provides that aircraft engaged on certain types of flight will be admitted by the parties into each other's territories without the imposition of the 'regulations, conditions or limitations' provided for in Article 5(2) of the Chicago Convention. Such flights include the following:

(a) Flights for the purpose of meeting humanitarian or emergency needs;
(b) Taxi-class passenger flights of occasional character on request, provided that the aircraft does not have a seating capacity of more than six passengers and provided that the destination is chosen by the hirer or hirers and no part of the capacity of the aircraft is resold to the public;
(c) Flights on which the entire space is hired by a single person (individual, firm, corporation or institution) for the carriage of his or its staff or merchandise, provided that no part of such space is resold;
(d) Single flights, no operator or group of operators being entitled under this sub-paragraph to more than one flight per month between the same two traffic centres for all aircraft available to him.

The Agreement also provides that:

the same treatment shall be accorded to aircraft engaged in either of the following activities:

(a) The transport of freight exclusively;
(b) The transport of passengers between regions which have no reasonably direct connection by scheduled air services.

In this case, however, it is provided that 'any contracting State may require the abandonment of the activities specified in this paragraph if it deems that these are harmful to the interests of its scheduled air services operating in the territories to which this Agreement applies'. Finally the Agreement contains provisions for simplifying the procedure for obtaining permission in those cases where permission is still required.

The Paris Agreement is significant, not only in itself, but also psychologically in that it has shown that it is possible to tackle on a multilateral basis even the commercial aspects of civil aviation. Hitherto, as we shall see, while it had not proved too difficult to obtain agreement on a fairly extensive scale so far as air navigation was concerned, the regulation of air transport had largely eluded a multilateral solution and had proved to be the subject of hard bargaining on a purely bilateral basis.

We must now, however, leave the area of non-scheduled flights and return to the intractable and far more important problem of 'scheduled international air services'. At Chicago it had been agreed to disagree on this issue and not to deal with it in the main Convention, save for the purely negative Article 6 which I have already mentioned. There were three main proposals.

(*a*) The United States campaigned for the principle of 'the freedom of the air', not in the sense that Fauchille used to understand that expression, but in a commercial sense. It was not proposed to tamper with the doctrine of the sovereignty of each State over its air space, but merely to modify that sovereignty by subjecting it to certain restrictions, which curiously enough became known as 'freedoms of the air'. There were five of these 'freedoms', and they were set out in the International Air Transport Agreement ('Five-Freedoms' Agreement) which the United States and a few other countries accepted at Chicago. This Agreement provided that:

Each contracting State grants to the other contracting States the following freedoms of the air in respect of scheduled international air services:
(1) The privilege to fly across its territory without landing;
(2) The privilege to land for non-traffic purposes;
(3) The privilege to put down passengers, mail and cargo taken on in the territory of the State whose nationality the aircraft possesses;
(4) The privilege to take on passengers, mail and cargo destined for the territory of the State whose nationality the aircraft possesses;
(5) The privilege to take on passengers, mail and cargo destined for the territory of any other contracting State and the privilege to put down passengers, mail and cargo coming from any such territory.

The United States, however, withdrew from this Agreement with effect from 25 July 1947, and since then it has been of little practical importance.

(*b*) At the other extreme, Australia and New Zealand championed the internationalization of commercial air transport.

(*c*) In the middle, the United Kingdom, supported by Canada, favoured what it chose to call 'order in the air'. According to this policy, countries would exchange the first four 'freedoms' multilaterally, but not the much more extensive 'fifth freedom'. Also, there would be an International Air Authority, which would have power to license operators and, in addition, to control the capacity provided and the rates charged.

It naturally proved impossible to reconcile such divergent views. Instead, as we have seen, the main Convention was silent on the question, and the United States and its supporters went ahead and introduced the 'Five-Freedoms' Agreement. The nearest approach to a compromise lay in the International Air Services Transit

65

Agreement ('Two-Freedoms' Agreement) which was accepted by many more countries (including the United Kingdom) than the 'Five-Freedoms' Agreement. Since this, however, covered the first two freedoms only—those dealing with 'transit', as opposed to 'traffic' rights—it did not really get to the heart of the controversy.

Basically, this controversy arises from the fact that some countries feel that the sovereignty which they possess over their land territory, and their air space, must in aviation matters be exploited for all that it is worth as an economic asset. If we may take as an example countries A, B and C, this means that A will not admit B's aircraft to its territory unless it can be sure that its own aircraft obtain a fair share of all third and fourth freedom traffic moving between A and B. Moreover, A will be suspicious of C's fifth freedom operations lest they impair A's own share of the traffic between A and other countries. There is the further difficulty of what constitutes a fair share. Take, for instance, the Netherlands and the United States. The Netherlands may feel that it is a fair bargain if half the passengers moving between these two countries go by KLM. But the United States may consider that that would be a very bad bargain for them since theirs is a far larger country with far more airports and a far larger number of their citizens travelling by air. In fact, it is because it has seen the proportion of the total traffic carried by American airlines steadily fall, especially in relation to the amount of traffic that is said to be 'generated' by the United States, that the United States, which appeared at Chicago as the champion of the freedoms of the air, has tended recently to adopt a more protectionist attitude. Conversely, a country such as the Netherlands, which has relatively little to bargain with as regards control of air space and the amount of traffic it 'generates', is now perhaps the strongest protagonist of freedom in civil aviation. In this the Dutch, who for centuries prospered on the maritime 'carrying trade', are only following their national tradition and seeking to obtain for civil aviation the same freedom of operation that shipping has hitherto enjoyed. But it is proving an uphill fight, and there are signs that, so far from civil aviation following the maritime example, many of the restrictive practices which have plagued civil aviation from its inception are now being extended to shipping.

There is, however, little that international law can do about this. Once the principle of national control over the air space and the admission of foreign aircraft is accepted, the exchange of air routes simply becomes a matter of bargaining. Nor is the bargaining limited to the balancing of one country's aviation interests against another's. The British Government, for instance, when negotiating aviation agreements with other countries, cannot afford to act solely as an agent for BOAC, BEA and other British airlines. While not neglecting such commercial interests, it must have regard to considerations of foreign policy as well. Since the exchange of air traffic rights as regards 'scheduled international air services' has become a matter of bilateral agreement, it would be tedious to pursue it further here, the more so as the task has been exhaustively carried out by Dr. Bin Cheng.[1] Brief reference must, however, be made to the agreement between the United Kingdom and the United States reached at Bermuda on 11 February 1946. Not merely did this Agreement heal the breach which appeared at Chicago, but the so-called 'Bermuda principles' have since been followed in countless other air services agreements, by other countries as well as by the United Kingdom and the United States themselves. The success of these principles is the more remarkable in that it is difficult to say with precision exactly what they amount to.

At Bermuda the two countries concerned concluded an agreement in which each granted to the other 'rights to the extent described in the Annex to this Agreement for the purpose of the establishment of air services described therein'. The routes set out in the Annex contained 'fifth-freedom' rights as well as the third and fourth freedoms. Thus United Kingdom air carriers were granted the right to fly from London to Hong Kong via New York, San Francisco and Manila; whilst United States carriers could fly from Chicago to Frankfurt via Shannon and London. The Americans also abandoned the hostility they had shown at Chicago to the control of rates and accepted the principle that rates could be fixed—subject to final Government approval—by the International Air Transport Association (IATA), an organization representing the leading airlines which was established in 1945 and which has its seat in Montreal, where the headquarters of ICAO is also located. Lastly, the two Governments tackled the thorny problem of capacity and the competitive position generally as between the airlines of the two countries. In the Final Act of the Conference they stressed the need for 'a fair and equal opportunity for the carriers of the two nations'; they asserted that 'in the operation by the air carriers of either Government of the trunk services described in the Annex to the Agreement, the interest

[1] *The Law of International Air Transport* (1962).

of the air carriers of the other Government shall be taken into consideration so as not to affect unduly the services which the latter provides on all or part of the same routes'; and they provided that, in so far as the carriers of one Government might be at a disadvantage due to the war, the situation should be 'reviewed between the Governments with the object of facilitating the necessary development, as soon as the air carrier or carriers of the first Government is or are in a position increasingly to make their proper contribution to the service'. All this was designed to set at rest the fears of the British Government whose civil aviation was in a sorry state immediately after the war. The parties also put on record the following remarkable formula:

That it is the understanding of both Governments that services provided by a designated air carrier under the Agreement and its Annex shall retain as their primary objective the provision of capacity adequate to the traffic demands between the country of which such air carrier is a national and the country of ultimate destination of the traffic. The right to embark or disembark on such services international traffic destined for and coming from third countries at a point or points on the routes specified in the Annex to the Agreement shall be applied in accordance with the general principles of orderly development to which both Governments subscribe and shall be subject to the general principle that capacity should be related:

(a) To traffic requirements between the country of origin and the countries of destination;
(b) To the requirements of through airline operation; and
(c) To the traffic requirements of the area through which the airline passes after taking account of local and regional services.

What this amounted to in practice was that the British Government was prepared to grant to American airlines limited 'fifth-freedom' facilities without insisting on a principle to which it had hitherto attached great importance—'the pre-determination of capacity'. The American airlines would be allowed to exploit these facilities provided they did not put on so much 'capacity' as seriously to impair the services operated by BOAC and BEA. In order to ensure that this did not happen, the two Governments stated that it was their intention that 'there should be regular and frequent consultation between their respective aeronautical authorities . . . and that there should thereby be close collaboration in the observance of the principles and the implementation of the provisions outlined herein and in the Agreement and its Annex'.

Although the documents in which they were embodied give the

impression of a 'gentleman's agreement' quite as much as of a formal treaty, the 'Bermuda principles' have stood the test of time. Even if legally imprecise, they have a firm basis in commercial common sense. As a result of the optimism caused by the Bermuda Agreement, a renewed effort was made at Geneva in 1947 to obtain a multilateral agreement in regard to 'scheduled international air services'. But the attempt failed, and in 1957 even the relatively homogeneous group of European countries who concluded amongst themselves the Paris Agreement in respect of non-scheduled services decided that, so far as scheduled services are concerned, there was no hope of reaching a multilateral solution.

To conclude the first part of this final lecture, it only remains to refer briefly to ICAO and to certain British legislation.

In such matters as prohibited areas and the conditions under which the aircraft of one country may fly into the air space of another, the provisions of the Chicago Convention follow very closely not merely the provisions of the Paris Convention (1919), but even the rules sketched out earlier by Fauchille. There is, however, one significant difference as compared with the Paris Convention. No longer are the technical matters dealt with in the annexes actually part of the Convention. Article 54 of the Chicago Convention indeed provides that one of the tasks of the Council of ICAO is to adopt 'international standards and recommended practices'; to designate these as annexes to the Convention; and to amend these annexes from time to time. But, under Article 37, the contracting States undertake only 'to collaborate in securing the highest practicable "degree of uniformity" in these matters', whilst Article 38 merely requires that 'any State which finds it impracticable to comply in all respects with any such international standard or procedure, or to bring its own regulations or practices into full accord with any international standard or procedure after amendment of the latter, or which deems it necessary to adopt regulations or practices differing in any particular respect from those established by an international standard, shall give immediate notification to the International Civil Aviation Organization of the differences between its own practice and that established by the international standard'. This is the price which ICAO has to pay for having a much larger membership than the old CINA. Needless to say, the members of ICAO vary enormously in aeronautical skills. However, the importance of uniformity is not lost sight of as Article 12 provides that 'over the high seas, the rules in force shall be those established under this Convention', and Chapter XV lays down a system whereby the Council of ICAO may help to improve air navigation facilities in the less advanced States, naturally with the consent of those States.

In order to enable the United Kingdom to become a party to the Chicago Convention, and for the purpose of regulating air navigation generally, Parliament passed the Air Navigation Act, 1947. This was followed by the Civil Aviation Act, 1949,[1] a most important piece of legislation which consolidated the law on this subject. In the same year Parliament passed the Air Corporations Act, which is the basic charter under which BOAC (originally established by the British Overseas Airways Act, 1939) and BEA (originally established by the Civil Aviation Act, 1946) still operate. At first the legislation of the post-war Labour Government left little scope for private enterprise in British civil aviation. For example, Section 24(1) of the Air Corporations Act, 1949, reserved to the State corporations and their associates the right 'to carry passengers or goods by air for hire or reward upon any scheduled journey between two places of which at least one is in the United Kingdom'. However, in a directive dated 26 January 1949, the Minister of Civil Aviation informed the Air Transport Advisory Council that it was Government policy to favour arrangements whereby private companies could, as 'associates' of the corporations, operate certain types of service, especially ferry, cross-country and seasonal services. In a directive dated 30 July 1952, the new Conservative Minister of Civil Aviation gave more scope to these companies, even allowing them to operate scheduled services in certain cases, although still as 'associates' of the corporations. By the Civil Aviation (Licensing) Act, 1960, Section 24(1) of the Air Corporations Act, 1949, was repealed, and the private companies were now allowed to go before the new Air Transport Licensing Board and apply for permission to operate air transport services on a level footing with the State corporations.

TRESPASSING IN AIR SPACE

A problem which has attracted much attention in recent years is that of trespassing in national air space by foreign aircraft. It is not a new problem. In 1904 Russian soldiers shot down a German balloon. The incident gave rise to considerable indignation, the more so as it was alleged that the balloon was not actually over Russian

[1] Section 40 of this Act substantially re-enacted Section 9 of the Air Navigation Act, 1920, as to which see p. 36.

territory at the time. Four years later at least ten German balloons carrying military officers crossed into France, and the desire to avoid such incidents in future seems to have been one of the reasons why the French Government sponsored the conference of 1910.

A number of incidents occurred between the two Wars. For instance, in January 1931, two Polish military aeroplanes landed in Germany. The leading pilot was sentenced to two weeks' imprisonment, but his companion was acquitted. Four months later, the German courts had to deal with a case in which a Polish military pilot, after landing in Germany by mistake and being informed by the local inhabitants that he was in Germany, endeavoured to fly back to Poland but had to land in German territory again because of lack of petrol. He was sentenced to three days' imprisonment for entering Germany illegally, and to seven days' detention for attempting to resume his flight without the permission of the German authorities. A few cases are also reported in which intruding aircraft were confiscated, but on the whole, by more recent standards, such aircraft seem to have been leniently treated in the inter-war period.

Some incidents that have taken place since 1945 have been more serious. It is only possible to consider a few of them here.

(i) On 19 August 1946, an unarmed American military transport aircraft was shot down over Yugoslavia. According to the Americans the aircraft had been forced into Yugoslavia unintentionally by bad weather and was shot down without warning. In a Note to Yugoslavia, the United States Government described the shooting down of the aircraft as an 'outrageous act', 'a plain violation of the obligations resting upon Yugoslavia under the Charter of the United Nations', and 'an offence against the law of nations and the principles of humanity'. To this strong language the Yugoslav Government replied that it accepted no legal liability. It asserted that the aircraft had flown over Yugoslavia illegally and had refused orders to land. When two Governments are at such variance over the facts, it is difficult to deduce legal principles from their correspondence, but it does seem that both parties were agreed that in time of peace intruding military aircraft should not be shot down without at least being given an opportunity to comply with orders to land.

(ii) On 13 June 1952, a Swedish military aeroplane was shot down by Soviet fighters over the Baltic. Again the facts were disputed, and a further complication concerned the actual extent of the Soviet air space, as the Soviet Union's claim to territorial waters of twelve miles—and consequently the air space above those waters—is not recognized by Sweden. Again the Notes exchanged reveal a general understanding that intruding military aircraft should be given an opportunity to land before being fired upon, although, according to the Swedish Note, there were 'fundamental differences' in the attitude of the two countries. As the Swedish Note puts it: 'While the instructions of the Swedish Air Force mean that the foreign aircraft is not fired upon if it changes its course and flies away, the Soviet instructions seem to imply that the foreign aircraft is fired upon if it flies away instead of landing.' This last factor, coupled with the Soviet Union's claim to territorial waters of twelve miles, probably helps to explain other incidents that have occurred in or near that country.

(iii) On 7 October 1952, a United States B29 aircraft was shot down by Soviet fighters between Yuri Island and Akiyuri Island. This was an area which, in the view of the United States, belonged to Japan, although the Soviet Government claimed that the aircraft had violated Soviet air space. Again it is obvious that disputed frontiers are particularly liable to generate aerial incidents. The United States referred the case to the International Court of Justice, but the latter, finding that the Soviet Government had not accepted the jurisdiction of the Court, ordered the case to be removed from the list.[1]

(iv) Similar incidents occurred on 4 September 1954 and on 7 November 1954. Again the United States referred the cases to the International Court of Justice, and again the Court had to order them to be removed from its list.[2]

(v) The United States also instituted proceedings before the Court against both Hungary and the Soviet Union concerning an American C47 military transport aircraft forced down by Soviet fighters over Hungary on 19 November 1951. The respondent States declined to accept jurisdiction, and again the Court had to remove the case from its list.[3] The same thing happened when the United States brought suit against Czechoslovakia over an aerial incident which occurred on 10 March 1953.[4]

(vi) An aerial incident which nearly led to the Court giving a judgement on the merits of the case was that which occurred on 27 July 1955. A Constellation aircraft belonging to El Al Israel Airlines Limited was shot down over Bulgaria while on a flight from Vienna

[1] I.C.J. Reports 1956, p. 9.
[2] I.C.J. Reports 1958, p. 158 and I.C.J. Reports 1959, p. 276.
[3] I.C.J. Reports 1954, pp. 99 and 103.
[4] I.C.J. Reports 1956, p. 6.

to Lydda. All the occupants, consisting of fifty-one passengers of varying nationalities, and seven crew members, also of varying nationalities, were killed. Israel asked the International Court of Justice to declare that Bulgaria was responsible under international law for the destruction of the aircraft and for the loss of life and property and all other damage that resulted therefrom, and also to determine the amount of compensation due from Bulgaria to Israel. Actions were also brought by the United States and the United Kingdom, which had lost respectively nine and four of their nationals. All the applicant States had some hope of persuading the Court to exercise jurisdiction, because on 29 July 1921 Bulgaria had signed— and had subsequently ratified—a declaration accepting the compulsory jurisdiction of the Statute of the Permanent Court of International Justice. Moreover, Article 36(5) of the Statute of the International Court of Justice provided as follows:

Declarations made under Article 36 of the Statute of the Permanent Court of International Justice and which are still in force shall be deemed, as between the parties to the present Statute, to be acceptances of the compulsory jurisdiction of the International Court of Justice for the period which they still have to run and in accordance with their terms.

The Bulgarian declaration had never been withdrawn. However, the Court held that the declaration was not caught by Article 36(5) because Bulgaria, although she became a party to the Statute of the Court on 14 December 1955, was not represented at the San Francisco Conference in 1945, when the present Statute was drafted. It was also held that, even if Article 36(5) did apply to the Bulgarian declaration, that declaration was no longer 'in force' since it must be deemed to have lapsed with the dissolution of the Permanent Court of International Justice in 1946.[1] The main Israeli action having failed, the cases brought by the United Kingdom and the United States were subsequently discontinued.[2]

(vii) Perhaps the best known of all incidents was that of the U2, piloted by Francis Gary Powers. On 1 May 1960, this high-flying United States reconnaissance plane was shot down near Sverdlovsk. This time there was no possible doubt that the plane was over Soviet territory, and intentionally so. After some hesitation, the United States Government, and even President Eisenhower himself, accepted responsibility for the flight. When the Soviet Union raised the matter in the Security Council, Ambassador Lodge gave as a justification

[1] *I.C.J. Reports 1959*, p. 127.
[2] *I.C.J. Reports 1959*, p. 264; and *I.C.J. Reports 1960*, p. 146.

for the flight the need for the free world to protect itself against a government 'well known for its expansionist activities and armed to the teeth'. Only Poland supported the Soviet draft resolution which would have the Council condemn 'the incursions by United States aircraft into other States' and regard these incursions as 'aggressive acts'. The draft resolution was consequently not carried.

(viii) Only slightly less well known is the case of the American RB 47 plane shot down by Soviet aircraft on 1 July 1960. This incident was more like the earlier ones in that the facts were disputed. The Soviet Union said that the American plane had penetrated Soviet air space and had refused to land when ordered to do so. The Americans stated that the plane had at no time been nearer than thirty miles to the Soviet coast. Again the Soviet draft resolution in the Security Council was supported only by Poland, whilst in its turn the Soviet Union vetoed an American resolution proposing that the case be referred either to a fact-finding commission or to the International Court of Justice.

(ix) United States planes have also been admitted for some time to be engaged in reconnaissance flights over Cuba, and one was shot down during the missile crisis of October 1962.

It is much to be regretted that, despite all these incidents, there has been no opportunity to advance the state of the law by judicial decision. Particularly is this true of the case involving the El Al airliner, because this case was not one with serious Cold War implications, such as surrounded the U2, RB 47 and Cuba reconnaissance flights. In all of these incidents the Governments concerned have put their views on record, and in the El Al case they had to formulate these views with the greater precision required when a case is presented to a court. There is, therefore, a good deal of material available for research, but it must be admitted that, while it is generally agreed that each State has sovereignty over its air space, considerable uncertainty still surrounds the exact procedure which should be followed when a plane involuntarily intrudes into foreign territory. As for deliberate unauthorized entry into foreign air space, this question involves the extent of the right of self-defence under modern international law—an issue beyond the scope of these lectures.

CRIME ON BOARD AIRCRAFT

Article 17 of the Chicago Convention provides that 'Aircraft have the nationality of the State in which they are registered'. What does it mean, though, to say that an aircraft has a 'nationality'? Does it mean that the State where it is registered can protect that aircraft should it be interfered with when flying over the high seas or in the air space of other States? Or does it mean that the aircraft is considered to be part of the territory of the State where it is registered, so that any act (e.g. a crime) committed on the aircraft is to be treated as if it took place on the territory of the State? Both these concepts are useful, so long as they are not pressed too far.

The shipping world has been much troubled recently by the problem of 'flags of convenience', i.e. the problem of ships owned by nationals of one State but registered in, and consequently flying the flag of, another State so as to obtain tax and other advantages there. A movement has developed to try to limit this practice. Thus, Article 5 of the Geneva Convention on the High Seas (1958) says: 'There must exist a genuine link between the State and the ship; in particular, the State must effectively exercise its jurisdiction and control in administrative, technical and social matters over ships flying its flag.' This problem has not yet become serious with regard to aircraft, although it is interesting that the 'Form of Standard Agreement' recommended at Chicago, as well as the 'Two-Freedoms' and 'Five-Freedoms' Agreements, all contain clauses authorizing the revocation of permits when a State is not satisfied that the airline to which it has granted a permit is under the 'substantial ownership and effective control' of nationals of the other contracting State.

In general, however, with aircraft as with ships, it is left to each State to determine the conditions on which it will admit such craft to its register. The suggestion made by Fauchille[1] that this matter should to some extent by governed by international rules has not been followed.

Briefly, the attitude of international law with regard to the exercise of jurisdiction over crimes is as follows. Each State may punish crimes committed on its own territory, whether by its own nationals or by foreigners. This is called jurisdiction according to the 'territorial principle'. Each State may also punish crimes committed anywhere by its own nationals. This is called jurisdiction according to the 'active nationality principle', and is in no way controversial. Some States, however, claim jurisdiction according to what is called the 'passive nationality principle'. This means that they arrogate to themselves the right to punish crimes, wherever committed, of which their own nationals are victims. Their right to do this is, however, disputed.

[1] Above, p. 12.

There are also certain other principles, such as the 'universal principle', which authorizes all States to punish crimes of a heinous nature which threaten the international community as a whole (e.g. piracy), or the 'protective principle', under which States may punish crimes, wherever committed, which directly threaten their own security.

In the law of the sea a practice has long been followed whereby, save for a few exceptions such as piracy, jurisdiction belongs exclusively to the State whose flag a ship flies so long as the ship is on the high seas. This means that, for the specific purpose of the exercise of criminal jurisdiction, the ship may be assimilated to territory. It does not mean that for all purposes the ship is so assimilated. When a vessel goes into foreign territorial waters, another State as well as the 'flag-State' immediately becomes concerned and a case of 'concurrent jurisdiction' may arise. International law is not particularly concerned about this: its role is to say when a State may exercise jurisdiction and when it may not, not to deal with possible conflicts of jurisdiction. In practice, this particular problem has been solved by the territorial State abstaining from the exercise of jurisdiction except in the case of particularly serious crimes.

This solution ('the law of the flag') was favoured for aircraft by Fauchille in his original code, although he would have allowed the subjacent State to deal with offences directly affecting it, such as espionage and breaches of customs regulations.[1] It is often argued that persons travelling in an aircraft, like those in a ship, constitute a community and that it is more realistic to let 'the law of the flag' regulate their activities than to have them regulated by the laws of the several States through whose air space they may happen to fly. Moreover, if 'the law of the flag' were not in charge, the community when over the high seas would be subject to no law at all. These are powerful arguments, but they do not prevail over all other considerations. Air journeys do not usually take as long as sea voyages. Aircraft spend far more time than ships do in the territories of other States. They are, in this respect, almost as much like trains and motor-coaches (for which a 'law of the flag' would be absurd) as they are like ships. The consequence is that, in considering crimes committed on board aircraft, the jurisdiction of the subjacent State must be provided for as well as that of the flag-State.

There is a further point. International law, as I have said, is mainly concerned with the question when a State should exercise jurisdiction

[1] Above, p. 13.

and when it should not. It cannot compel States to exercise jurisdiction when they lack power to do so under their own laws. As we saw in the first lecture, this situation happened with regard to a ship in the English courts in *The Queen* v. *Keyn*.[1] It has also happened on some occasions with regard to aircraft. In *United States* v. *Cordova*,[2] the District Court for the Eastern District of New York found itself without jurisdiction to punish a man charged with assaulting the pilot, the stewardess and another passenger even in an American aircraft flying over the high seas between Puerto Rico and New York. In order to remedy this deficiency Congress passed a statute in 1952 and, as spectacular aircraft crimes (notably 'hi-jacking') continued to take place, the law was strengthened in 1961.

In *Regina* v. *Martin*,[3] Mr. Justice Devlin (as he then was) had to interpret an awkward section (Section 62(1)) of the Civil Aviation Act, 1949, which read as follows:

Any offence whatever committed on a British aircraft shall, for the purpose of conferring jurisdiction, be deemed to have been committed in any place where the offender may for the time being be.

Certain persons were charged with an offence under some regulations made under the Dangerous Drugs Act, 1951, in that they were in possession of raw opium on a British aircraft flying between Bahrain and Singapore. Devlin, J., interpreted Section 62(1) as a 'venue-creating' rather than an 'offence-creating' section. If the act with which the accused were charged were an offence when committed on board a British aircraft, then the court would have jurisdiction; but otherwise not. In his view, offences under the Dangerous Drugs Act were offences only if committed in Great Britain itself. Therefore the court lacked jurisdiction. Devlin, J., warned, however, that the position might be different as regards common law crimes, such as murder and theft, which, in his view, were crimes wherever they were committed.

The question whether a British aircraft is part of British territory also came before a Commissioner under the National Insurance Acts. A BOAC aircraft flying between the United States and Great Britain had to turn back to Gander, Newfoundland, because of engine trouble. A passenger became ill and had to incur hospital expenses in Newfoundland. He claimed that he was entitled to sickness benefit under a regulation which provides that a person shall not be

---

[1] [1876] 2 Ex. D. 63. Above, p. 2.   [2] (1950) 89 F. Supp. 298.
[3] [1956] 2 Q.B. 272.

disqualified if he can prove that his absence from Great Britain is a temporary one for the specific purpose of being treated for incapacity which commenced before he left Great Britain. The only hope of avoiding the disqualification lay in showing that the British aircraft constituted British territory. But the Commissioner disallowed the claim saying there was nothing to warrant his holding that 'an aeroplane flying over the high seas, even though British owned, is any part of Great Britain'.[1] In *Regina* v. *Naylor*[2] Lord Parker, C.J., had to consider a case which bore some resemblance to *Regina* v. *Martin*. A girl was charged with stealing three rings on a British aircraft in flight over the high seas. It was argued on her behalf that that was not an offence known to English law, and so she could not be tried. Referring to the fact that, in the earlier case, Devlin, J., had expressly mentioned theft as a crime not having territorial limits, Lord Parker, C.J., went on to make it clear that in any event he took a rather broader view of Section 62(1) than Devlin, J., had done. Admitting that the language of the Section was 'unfortunate', he nevertheless said:

In my judgement, the approach to this matter is that any act or omission which would constitute an offence if done in England is made an offence if done on a British aircraft, subject to this; if the offence in question is clearly one of domestic application only, then, as in *Regina* v. *Martin*, Section 62(1) does not cover that sort of offence.

This decision put at rest fears that lawlessness might prevail on British aircraft. But the problems of crimes committed on board aircraft remains a difficult one. There are so many complications, ranging from political issues such as extradition and the right of asylum at one extreme to the practical problem of keeping obstreperous persons in custody on board aircraft or at airports at the other, that an international solution is essential. In this respect the Convention on Offences and certain Other Acts Committed on board Aircraft, signed at Tokyo on 14 September 1963, represents a step on the road towards a more mature and comprehensive law of the air. The Convention will come into force upon being ratified by twelve States.[3] The Convention is wisely concerned not merely with crimes but with all 'acts which, whether or not they are offences, may or do jeopardize the safety of the aircraft or of persons or property therein or which jeopardize good order and discipline on board' (Article 1(1)). Basic-

[1] *International Law Reports*, Vol. 27, p. 115.
[2] [1962] 2 Q.B. 527. See also *Cox* v. *Army Council* [1963] A.C. 48.
[3] The text of the Convention is printed at Appendix I.

ally the Convention provides for the operation of 'the law of the flag', e.g. 'The State of registration of the aircraft is competent to exercise jurisdiction over offences and acts committed on board' (Article 3(1)). But Article 4 provides also for the exercise of jurisdiction according to the territorial principle, the active nationality principle, the passive nationality principle, the protective principle and the universal principle. So there is a danger that, whereas in the past there has sometimes been insufficient jurisdiction with regard to crimes committed on board aircraft, there may in the future be too much. But there will be a welcome for the attempt to stamp out 'hi-jacking' contained in Article 11(1) which provides as follows:

When a person on board has unlawfully committed by force or threat thereof an act of interference, seizure, or other wrongful exercise of control of an aircraft in flight or when such an act is about to be committed, Contracting States shall take all appropriate measures to restore control of the aircraft to its lawful commander or to preserve his control of the aircraft.

Appendix I

CONVENTION ON OFFENCES AND CERTAIN OTHER ACTS COMMITTED ON BOARD AIRCRAFT

(*Concluded at Tokyo on 14 September 1963*)

THE STATES Parties to this Convention
HAVE AGREED as follows:

CHAPTER I—SCOPE OF THE CONVENTION

ARTICLE 1

1. This Convention shall apply in respect of:

(*a*) offences against penal law;

(*b*) acts which, whether or not they are offences, may or do jeopardize the safety of the aircraft or of persons or property therein or which jeopardize good order and discipline on board.

2. Except as provided in Chapter III, this Convention shall apply in respect of offences committed or acts done by a person on board any aircraft registered in a Contracting State, while that aircraft is in flight or on the surface of the high seas or of any other area outside the territory of any State.

3. For the purposes of this Convention, an aircraft is considered to be in flight from the moment when power is applied for the purpose of take-off until the moment when the landing run ends.

4. This Convention shall not apply to aircraft used in military, customs or police services.

ARTICLE 2

Without prejudice to the provisions of Article 4 and except when the safety of the aircraft or of persons or property on board so requires, no provision of this Convention shall be interpreted as authorizing or requiring any action in respect of offences against penal laws of a political nature or those based on racial or religious discrimination.

CHAPTER II—JURISDICTION

ARTICLE 3

1. The State of registration of the aircraft is competent to exercise jurisdiction over offences and acts committed on board.

2. Each Contracting State shall take such measures as may be necessary to establish its jurisdiction as the State of registration over offences committed on board aircraft registered in such State.

3. This Convention does not exclude any criminal jurisdiction exercised in accordance with national law.

ARTICLE 4

A Contracting State which is not the State of registration may not interfere with an aircraft in flight in order to exercise its criminal jurisdiction over an offence committed on board except in the following cases:

(a) the offence has effect on the territory of such State;

(b) the offence has been committed by or against a national or permanent resident of such State;

(c) the offence is against the security of such State;

(d) the offence consists of a breach of any rules or regulations relating to the flight or manœuvre of aircraft in force in such State;

(e) the exercise of jurisdiction is necessary to ensure the observance of any obligation of such State under a multilateral international agreement.

CHAPTER III—POWERS OF THE AIRCRAFT COMMANDER

ARTICLE 5

1. The provisions of this Chapter shall not apply to offences and acts committed or about to be committed by a person on board an aircraft in flight in the airspace of the State of registration or over the high seas or any other area outside the territory of any State unless the last point of take-off or the next point of intended landing is situated in a State other than that of registration, or the aircraft subsequently flies in the airspace of a State other than that of registration with such person still on board.

2. Notwithstanding the provisions of Article 1, paragraph 3, an aircraft shall for the purposes of this Chapter, be considered to be in flight at any time from the moment when all its external doors are closed following embarkation until the moment when any such door is opened for disembarkation. In the case of a forced landing, the provisions of this Chapter shall continue to apply with respect to offences and acts committed on board until competent authorities of a State take over the responsibility for the aircraft and for the persons and property on board.

ARTICLE 6

1. The aircraft commander may, when he has reasonable grounds to believe that a person has committed, or is about to commit, on board the aircraft, an offence or act contemplated in Article 1, paragraph 1, impose

81

upon such person reasonable measures including restraint which are necessary:

(a) to protect the safety of the aircraft, or of persons or property therein; or

(b) to maintain good order and discipline on board; or

(c) to enable him to deliver such person to competent authorities or to disembark him in accordance with the provisions of this Chapter.

2. The aircraft commander may require or authorize the assistance of other crew members and may request or authorize, but not require, the assistance of passengers to restrain any person whom he is entitled to restrain. Any crew member or passenger may also take reasonable preventive measures without such authorization when he has reasonable grounds to believe that such action is immediately necessary to protect the safety of the aircraft, or of persons or property therein.

ARTICLE 7

1. Measures of restraint imposed upon a person in accordance with Article 6 shall not be continued beyond any point at which the aircraft lands unless:

(a) such point is in the territory of a non-Contracting State and its authorities refuse to permit disembarkation of that person or those measures have been imposed in accordance with Article 6, paragraph 1(c) in order to enable his delivery to competent authorities;

(b) the aircraft makes a forced landing and the aircraft commander is unable to deliver that person to competent authorities; or

(c) that person agrees to onward carriage under restraint.

2. The aircraft commander shall as soon as practicable, and if possible before landing in the territory of a State with a person on board who has been placed under restraint in accordance with the provisions of Article 6, notify the authorities of such State of the fact that a person on board is under restraint and of the reasons for such restraint.

ARTICLE 8

1. The aircraft commander may, in so far as it is necessary for the purpose of subparagraph (a) or (b) of paragraph 1 of Article 6, disembark in the territory of any State in which the aircraft lands any person who he has reasonable grounds to believe has committed, or is about to commit, on board the aircraft an act contemplated in Article 1, paragraph 1(b).

2. The aircraft commander shall report to the authorities of the State in which he disembarks any person pursuant to this Article, the fact of, and the reasons for, such disembarkation.

ARTICLE 9

1. The aircraft commander may deliver to the competent authorities of any Contracting State in the territory of which the aircraft lands any

person who he has reasonable grounds to believe has committed on board the aircraft an act which, in his opinion, is a serious offence according to the penal law of the State of registration of the aircraft.

2. The aircraft commander shall as soon as practicable and if possible before landing in the territory of a Contracting State with a person on board whom the aircraft commander intends to deliver in accordance with the preceding paragraph, notify the authorities of such State of his intention to deliver such person and the reasons therefor.

3. The aircraft commander shall furnish the authorities to whom any suspected offender is delivered in accordance with the provisions of this Article with evidence and information which, under the law of the State of registration of the aircraft, are lawfully in his possession.

ARTICLE 10

For actions taken in accordance with this Convention, neither the aircraft commander, any other member of the crew, any passenger, the owner or operator of the aircraft, nor the person on whose behalf the flight was performed shall be held responsible in any proceeding on account of the treatment undergone by the person against whom the actions were taken.

CHAPTER IV—UNLAWFUL SEIZURE OF AIRCRAFT

ARTICLE 11

1. When a person on board has unlawfully committed by force or threat thereof an act of interference, seizure, or other wrongful exercise of control of an aircraft in flight or when such an act is about to be committed, Contracting States shall take all appropriate measures to restore control of the aircraft to its lawful commander or to preserve his control of the aircraft

2. In the cases contemplated in the preceding paragraph, the Contracting State in which the aircraft lands shall permit its passengers and crew to continue their journey as soon as practicable, and shall return the aircraft and its cargo to the persons lawfully entitled to possession.

CHAPTER V—POWERS AND DUTIES OF STATES

ARTICLE 12

Any Contracting State shall allow the commander of an aircraft registered in another Contracting State to disembark any person pursuant to Article 8, paragraph 1.

ARTICLE 13

1. Any Contracting State shall take delivery of any person whom the aircraft commander delivers pursuant to Article 9, paragraph 1.

2. Upon being satisfied that the circumstances so warrant, any Contracting State shall take custody or other measures to ensure the presence of any person suspected of an act contemplated in Article 11, paragraph 1, and of any person of whom it has taken delivery. The custody and other measures shall be as provided in the law of that State but may only be continued for such time as is reasonably necessary to enable any criminal or extradition proceedings to be instituted.

3. Any person in custody pursuant to the previous paragraph shall be assisted in communicating immediately with the nearest appropriate representative of the State of which he is a national.

4. Any Contracting State, to which a person is delivered pursuant to Article 9, paragraph 1, or in whose territory an aircraft lands following the commission of an act contemplated in Article 11, paragraph 1, shall immediately make a preliminary enquiry into the facts.

5. When a State, pursuant to this Article, has taken a person into custody, it shall immediately notify the State of registration of the aircraft and the State of nationality of the detained person and, if it considers it advisable, any other interested State of the fact that such person is in custody and of the circumstances which warrant his detention. The State which makes the preliminary enquiry contemplated in paragraph 4 of this Article shall promptly report its findings to the said States and shall indicate whether it intends to exercise jurisdiction.

ARTICLE 14

1. When any person has been disembarked in accordance with Article 8, paragraph 1, or delivered in accordance with Article 9, paragraph 1, or has disembarked after committing an act contemplated in Article 11, paragraph 1, and when such person cannot or does not desire to continue his journey and the State of landing refuses to admit him, that State may, if the person in question is not a national or permanent resident of that State, return him to the territory of the State of which he is a national or permanent resident or to the territory of the State in which he began his journey by air.

2. Neither disembarkation, nor delivery, nor the taking of custody or other measures contemplated in Article 13, paragraph 2, nor return of the person concerned, shall be considered as admission to the territory of the Contracting State concerned for the purpose of its law relating to entry or admission of persons and nothing in this Convention shall affect the law of a Contracting State relating to the expulsion of persons from its territory.

ARTICLE 15

1. Without prejudice to Article 14, any person who has been disembarked in accordance with Article 8, paragraph 1, or delivered in accordance with Article 9, paragraph 1, or has disembarked after committing an act contemplated in Article 11, paragraph 1, and who desires to continue his journey shall be at liberty as soon as practicable to proceed to any destination of his choice unless his presence is required by the law of the State of landing for the purpose of extradition or criminal proceedings.

2. Without prejudice to its law as to entry and admission to, and extradition and expulsion from its territory, a Contracting State in whose territory a person has been disembarked in accordance with Article 8, paragraph 1, or delivered in accordance with Article 9, paragraph 1, or has disembarked and is suspected of having committed an act contemplated in Article 11, paragraph 1, shall accord to such person treatment which is no less favourable for his protection and security than that accorded to nationals of such Contracting State in like circumstances.

CHAPTER VI—OTHER PROVISIONS

ARTICLE 16

1. Offences committed on aircraft registered in a Contracting State shall be treated, for the purpose of extradition, as if they had been committed not only in the place in which they have occurred but also in the territory of the State of registration of the aircraft.
2. Without prejudice to the provisions of the preceding paragraph, nothing in this Convention shall be deemed to create an obligation to grant extradition.

ARTICLE 17

In taking any measures for investigation or arrest or otherwise exercising jurisdiction in connection with any offence committed on board an aircraft the Contracting States shall pay due regard to the safety and other interests of air navigation and shall so act as to avoid unnecessary delay of the aircraft, passengers, crew or cargo.

ARTICLE 18

If Contracting States establish joint air transport operating organizations or international operating agencies, which operate aircraft not registered in any one State, those States shall, according to the circumstances of the case, designate the State among them which, for the purposes of this Convention, shall be considered as the State of registration and shall give notice thereof to the International Civil Aviation Organization which shall communicate the notice to all States Parties to this Convention.

CHAPTER VII—FINAL CLAUSES

ARTICLE 19

Until the date on which this Convention comes into force in accordance with the provisions of Article 21, it shall remain open for signature on behalf of any State which at that date is a Member of the United Nations or of any of the Specialized Agencies.

ARTICLE 20

1. This Convention shall be subject to ratification by the signatory States in accordance with their constitutional procedures.

2. The instruments of ratification shall be deposited with the International Civil Aviation Organization.

ARTICLE 21

1. As soon as twelve of the signatory States have deposited their instruments of ratification of this Convention, it shall come into force between them on the ninetieth day after the date of the deposit of the twelfth instrument of ratification. It shall come into force for each State ratifying thereafter on the ninetieth day after the deposit of its instrument of ratification.

2. As soon as this Convention comes into force, it shall be registered with the Secretary-General of the United Nations by the International Civil Aviation Organization.

ARTICLE 22

1. This Convention shall, after it has come into force, be open for accession by any State Member of the United Nations or of any of the Specialized Agencies.

2. The accession of a State shall be effected by the deposit of an instrument of accession with the International Civil Aviation Organization and shall take effect on the ninetieth day after the date of such deposit.

ARTICLE 23

1. Any Contracting State may denounce this Convention by notification addressed to the International Civil Aviation Organization.

2. Denunciation shall take effect six months after the date of receipt by the International Civil Aviation Organization of the notification of denunciation.

ARTICLE 24

1. Any dispute between two or more Contracting States concerning the interpretation or application of this Convention which cannot be settled through negotiation, shall, at the request of one of them, be submitted to arbitration. If within six months from the date of the request for arbitration the Parties are unable to agree on the organization of the arbitration, any one of those Parties may refer the dispute to the International Court of Justice by request in conformity with the Statute of the Court.

2. Each State may at the time of signature or ratification of this Convention or accession thereto, declare that it does not consider itself bound by the preceding paragraph. The other Contracting States shall not be bound by the preceding paragraph with respect to any Contracting State having made such a reservation.

3. Any Contracting State having made a reservation in accordance with the preceding paragraph may at any time withdraw this reservation by notification to the International Civil Aviation Organization.

ARTICLE 25

Except as provided in Article 24 no reservation may be made to this Convention.

ARTICLE 26

The International Civil Aviation Organization shall give notice to all States Members of the United Nations or of any of the Specialized Agencies:

(a) of any signature of this Convention and the date thereof;
(b) of the deposit of any instrument of ratification or accession and the date thereof;
(c) of the date on which this Convention comes into force in accordance with Article 21, paragraph 1;
(d) of the receipt of any notification of denunciation and the date thereof; and
(e) of the receipt of any declaration or notification made under Article 24 and the date thereof.

IN WITNESS WHEREOF the undersigned Plenipotentiaries, having been duly authorized, have signed this Convention.

DONE at Tokyo on the fourteenth day of September One Thousand Nine Hundred and Sixty-three in three authentic texts drawn up in the English, French and Spanish languages.

This Convention shall be deposited with the International Civil Aviation Organization with which, in accordance with Article 19, it shall remain open for signature and the said Organization shall send certified copies thereof to all States Members of the United Nations or of any Specialized Agency.

[Here follow the signatures on behalf of the United Kingdom of Great Britain and Northern Ireland, Congo (Brazzaville), Federal Republic of Germany, Guatemala, Holy See, Indonesia, Italy, Japan, Liberia, Panama, Philippines, Republic of China, Republic of the Upper Volta, Sweden, United States of America, Yugoslavia.]

Appendix II

(A) TEXT OF THE CHICAGO CONVENTION, 1944

(B) LIST OF PARTIES TO THE CONVENTION

(A) CONVENTION ON INTERNATIONAL CIVIL AVIATION

(Signed at Chicago on 7 December 1944[1])

PREAMBLE

WHEREAS the future development of international civil aviation can greatly help to create and preserve friendship and understanding among the nations and peoples of the world, yet its abuse can become a threat to general security; and

WHEREAS it is desirable to avoid friction and to promote that cooperation between nations and peoples upon which the peace of the world depends;

THEREFORE, the undersigned governments having agreed on certain principles and arrangements in order that international civil aviation may be developed in a safe and orderly manner and that international air transport services may be established on the basis of equality of opportunity and operated soundly and economically;

Have accordingly concluded this Convention to that end.

PART I

AIR NAVIGATION

CHAPTER I—GENERAL PRINCIPLES AND APPLICATION OF THE CONVENTION

ARTICLE 1

Sovereignty

The contracting States recognize that every State has complete and exclusive sovereignty over the air space above its territory.

---

[1] Came into force on 4 April 1947, the thirtieth day after deposit with the Government of the United States of America of the twenty-sixth instrument of ratification thereof or notification of adherence thereto, in accordance with Article 91 (*b*).

ARTICLE 2

Territory

For the purposes of this Convention the territory of a State shall be deemed to be the land areas and territorial waters adjacent thereto under the sovereignty, suzerainty, protection or mandate of such State.

ARTICLE 3

Civil and state aircraft

(a) This Convention shall be applicable only to civil aircraft, and shall not be applicable to state aircraft.

(b) Aircraft used in military, customs and police services shall be deemed to be state aircraft.

(c) No state aircraft of a contracting State shall fly over the territory of another State or land thereon without authorization by special agreement or otherwise, and in accordance with the terms thereof.

(d) The contracting States undertake, when issuing regulations for their state aircraft, that they will have due regard for the safety of navigation of civil aircraft.

ARTICLE 4

Misuse of civil aviation

Each contracting State agrees not to use civil aviation for any purpose inconsistent with the aims of this Convention.

CHAPTER II—FLIGHT OVER TERRITORY OF CONTRACTING STATES

ARTICLE 5

Right of non-scheduled flight

Each contracting State agrees that all aircraft of the other contracting States, being aircraft not engaged in scheduled international air service, shall have the right, subject to the observance of the terms of this Convention, to make flights into or in transit non-stop across its territory and to make stops for non-traffic purposes without the necessity of obtaining prior permission, and subject to the right of the State flown over to require landing. Each contracting State nevertheless reserves the right, for reasons of safety of flight, to require aircraft desiring to proceed over regions which are inaccessible or without adequate air navigation facilities to follow prescribed routes, or to obtain special permission for such flights.

Such aircraft, if engaged in the carriage of passengers, cargo, or mail for remuneration or hire on other than scheduled international air services, shall also, subject to the provisions of Article 7, have the privilege of taking on or discharging passengers, cargo, or mail, subject to the right of any State where such embarkation or discharge takes place to

G

impose such regulations, conditions or limitations as it may consider desirable.

ARTICLE 6

Scheduled air services

No scheduled international air service may be operated over or into the territory of a contracting State, except with the special permission or other authorization of that State, and in accordance with the terms of such permission or authorization.

ARTICLE 7

Cabotage

Each contracting State shall have the right to refuse permission to the aircraft of other contracting States to take on in its territory passengers, mail and cargo carried for remuneration or hire and destined for another point within its territory. Each contracting State undertakes not to enter into any arrangements which specifically grant any such privilege on an exclusive basis to any other State or an airline of any other State, and not to obtain any such exclusive privilege from any other State.

ARTICLE 8

Pilotless aircraft

No aircraft capable of being flown without a pilot shall be flown without a pilot over the territory of a contracting State without special authorization by that State and in accordance with the terms of such authorization. Each contracting State undertakes to insure that the flight of such aircraft without a pilot in regions open to civil aircraft shall be so controlled as to obviate danger to civil aircraft.

ARTICLE 9

Prohibited areas

(*a*) Each contracting State may, for reasons of military necessity or public safety, restrict or prohibit uniformly the aircraft of other States from flying over certain areas of its territory, provided that no distinction in this respect is made between the aircraft of the State whose territory is involved, engaged in international scheduled airline services, and the aircraft of the other contracting States likewise engaged. Such prohibited areas shall be of reasonable extent and location so as not to interfere unnecessarily with air navigation. Descriptions of such prohibited areas in the territory of a contracting State, as well as any subsequent alterations therein, shall be communicated as soon as possible to the other contracting States and to the International Civil Aviation Organization.

(*b*) Each contracting State reserves also the right, in exceptional circumstances or during a period of emergency, or in the interest of public safety, and with immediate effect, temporarily to restrict or prohibit flying over the whole or any part of its territory, on condition that such restriction or prohibition shall be applicable without distinction of nationality to aircraft of all other States.

(*c*) Each contracting State, under such regulations as it may prescribe, may require any aircraft entering the areas contemplated in subparagraphs (*a*) or (*b*) above to effect a landing as soon as practicable thereafter at some designated airport within its territory.

ARTICLE 10

Landing at customs airport

Except in a case where, under the terms of this Convention or a special authorization, aircraft are permitted to cross the territory of a contracting State without landing, every aircraft which enters the territory of a contracting State shall, if the regulations of that State so require, land at an airport designated by that State for the purpose of customs and other examination. On departure from the territory of a contracting State, such aircraft shall depart from a similarly designated customs airport. Particulars of all designated customs airports shall be published by the State and transmitted to the International Civil Aviation Organization established under Part II of this Convention for communication to all other contracting States.

ARTICLE 11

Applicability of air regulations

Subject to the provisions of this Convention, the laws and regulations of a contracting State relating to the admission to or departure from its territory of aircraft engaged in international air navigation, or to the operation and navigation of such aircraft while within its territory, shall be applied to the aircraft of all contracting States without distinction as to nationality, and shall be complied with by such aircraft upon entering or departing from or while within the territory of that State.

ARTICLE 12

Rules of the air

Each contracting State undertakes to adopt measures to insure that every aircraft flying over or manœuvring within its territory and that every aircraft carrying its nationality mark, wherever such aircraft may be, shall comply with the rules and regulations relating to the flight and manœuvre of aircraft there in force. Each contracting State undertakes to keep its own regulations in these respects uniform, to the greatest possible extent, with those established from time to time under this Convention. Over the high seas, the rules in force shall be those established under this Convention. Each contracting State undertakes to insure the prosecution of all persons violating the regulations applicable.

ARTICLE 13

Entry and clearance regulations

The laws and regulations of a contracting State as to the admission to or departure from its territory of passengers, crew or cargo of aircraft, such as regulations relating to entry, clearance, immigration, passports, customs, and quarantine shall be complied with by or on behalf of such passengers, crew or cargo upon entrance into or departure from, or while within the territory of that State.

ARTICLE 14

Prevention of spread of disease

Each contracting State agrees to take effective measures to prevent the spread by means of air navigation of cholera, typhus (epidemic), smallpox, yellow fever, plague, and such other communicable diseases as the contracting States shall from time to time decide to designate, and to that end contracting States will keep in close consultation with the agencies concerned with international regulations relating to sanitary measures applicable to aircraft. Such consultation shall be without prejudice to the application of any existing international convention on this subject to which the contracting States may be parties.

ARTICLE 15

Airport and similar charges

Every airport in a contracting State which is open to public use by its national aircraft shall likewise, subject to the provisions of Article 68, be open under uniform conditions to the aircraft of all the other contracting States. The like uniform conditions shall apply to the use, by aircraft of every contracting State, of all air navigation facilities, including radio and meteorological services, which may be provided for public use for the safety and expedition of air navigation.

Any charges that may be imposed or permitted to be imposed by a contracting State for the use of such airports and air navigation facilities by the aircraft of any other contracting State shall not be higher,

(*a*) As to aircraft not engaged in scheduled international air services, than those that would be paid by its national aircraft of the same class engaged in similar operations, and

(*b*) As to aircraft engaged in scheduled international air services, than those that would be paid by its national aircraft engaged in similar international air services.

All such charges shall be published and communicated to the International Civil Aviation Organization: provided that, upon representation by an interested contracting State, the charges imposed for the use of airports and other facilities shall be subject to review by the Council, which shall report and make recommendations thereon for the consideration of the

State or States concerned. No fees, dues or other charges shall be imposed by any contracting State in respect solely of the right of transit over or entry into or exit from its territory of any aircraft of a contracting State or persons or property thereon.

ARTICLE 16

Search of aircraft

The appropriate authorities of each of the contracting States shall have the right, without unreasonable delay, to search aircraft of the other contracting States on landing or departure, and to inspect the certificates and other documents prescribed by the Convention.

CHAPTER III—NATIONALITY OF AIRCRAFT

ARTICLE 17

Nationality of aircraft

Aircraft have the nationality of the State in which they are registered.

ARTICLE 18

Dual registration

An aircraft cannot be validly registered in more than one State, but its registration may be changed from one State to another.

ARTICLE 19

National laws governing registration

The registration or transfer of registration of aircraft in any contracting State shall be made in accordance with its laws and regulations.

ARTICLE 20

Display of marks

Every aircraft engaged in international air navigation shall bear its appropriate nationality and registration marks.

ARTICLE 21

Report of registrations

Each contracting State undertakes to supply to any other contracting State or to the International Civil Aviation Organization, on demand, information concerning the registration and ownership of any particular aircraft registered in that State. In addition, each contracting State shall furnish reports to the International Civil Aviation Organization, under such regulations as the latter may prescribe, giving such pertinent data as can be made available concerning the ownership and control of aircraft registered in that State and habitually engaged in international air navigation. The data thus obtained by the International Civil Aviation Organization shall be made available by it on request to the other contracting States.

CHAPTER IV—MEASURES TO FACILITATE AIR NAVIGATION

ARTICLE 22

Facilitation of formalities

Each contracting State agrees to adopt all practicable measures, through the issuance of special regulations or otherwise, to facilitate and expedite navigation by aircraft between the territories of contracting States, and to prevent unnecessary delays to aircraft, crews, passengers and cargo, especially in the administration of the laws relating to immigration, quarantine, customs and clearance.

ARTICLE 23

Customs and immigration procedures

Each contracting State undertakes, so far as it may find practicable, to establish customs and immigration procedures affecting international air navigation in accordance with the practices which may be established or recommended from time to time, pursuant to this Convention. Nothing in this Convention shall be construed as preventing the establishment of customs-free airports.

ARTICLE 24

Customs duty

(*a*) Aircraft on a flight to, from, or across the territory of another contracting State shall be admitted temporarily free of duty, subject to the customs regulations of the State. Fuel, lubricating oils, spare parts, regular equipment and aircraft stores on board an aircraft of a contracting State, on arrival in the territory of another contracting State and retained on board on leaving the territory of that State shall be exempt from customs duty, inspection fees or similar national or local duties and charges. This exemption shall not apply to any quantities or articles unloaded, except in accordance with the customs regulations of the State, which may require that they shall be kept under customs supervision.

(*b*) Spare parts and equipment imported into the territory of a contracting State for incorporation in or use on an aircraft of another contracting State engaged in international air navigation shall be admitted free of customs duty, subject to compliance with the regulations of the State concerned, which may provide that the articles shall be kept under customs supervision and control.

ARTICLE 25

Aircraft in distress

Each contracting State undertakes to provide such measures of assistance to aircraft in distress in its territory as it may find practicable, and to permit, subject to control by its own authorities, the owners of the aircraft or authorities of the State in which the aircraft is registered to provide such measures of assistance as may be necessitated by the circumstances. Each contracting State, when undertaking search for missing aircraft, will collaborate in coordinated measures which may be recommended from time to time pursuant to this Convention.

ARTICLE 26

Investigation of accidents

In the event of an accident to an aircraft of a contracting State occurring in the territory of another contracting State, and involving death or serious injury, or indicating serious technical defect in the aircraft or air navigation facilities, the State in which the accident occurs will institute an inquiry into the circumstances of the accident, in accordance, so far as its laws permit, with the procedure which may be recommended by the International Civil Aviation Organization. The State in which the aircraft is registered shall be given the opportunity to appoint observers to be present at the inquiry and the State holding the inquiry shall communicate the report and findings in the matter to that State.

ARTICLE 27

Exemption from seizure on patent claims

(*a*) While engaged in international air navigation, any authorized entry of aircraft of a contracting State into the territory of another contracting State or authorized transit across the territory of such State with or without landings shall not entail any seizure or detention of the aircraft or any claim against the owner or operator thereof or any other interference therewith by or on behalf of such State or any person therein, on the ground that the construction, mechanism, parts, accessories or operation of the aircraft is an infringement of any patent, design, or model duly granted or registered in the State whose territory is entered by the aircraft, it being agreed that no deposit of security in connection with the foregoing exemption from seizure or detention of the aircraft shall in any case be required in the State entered by such aircraft.

(*b*) The provisions of paragraph (*a*) of this Article shall also be applicable to the storage of spare parts and spare equipment for the aircraft and the right to use and install the same in the repair of an aircraft of a contracting State in the territory of any other contracting State, provided that any patented part or equipment so stored shall not be sold or distributed internally in or exported commercially from the contracting State entered by the aircraft.

(*c*) The benefits of this Article shall apply only to such States, parties to

95

this Convention, as either (1) are parties to the International Convention for the Protection of Industrial Property and to any amendments thereof; or (2) have enacted patent laws which recognize and give adequate protection to inventions made by the nationals of the other States parties to this Convention.

ARTICLE 28

Air navigation facilities and standard systems

Each contracting State undertakes, so far as it may find practicable, to:

(a) Provide, in its territory, airports, radio services, meteorological services and other air navigation facilities to facilitate international air navigation, in accordance with the standards and practices recommended or established from time to time, pursuant to this Convention;

(b) Adopt and put into operation the appropriate standard systems of communications procedure, codes, markings, signals, lighting and other operational practices and rules which may be recommended or established from time to time, pursuant to this Convention;

(c) Collaborate in international measures to secure the publication of aeronautical maps and charts in accordance with standards which may be recommended or established from time to time, pursuant to this Convention.

CHAPTER V—CONDITIONS TO BE FULFILLED WITH RESPECT TO AIRCRAFT

ARTICLE 29

Documents carried in aircraft

Every aircraft of a contracting State, engaged in international navigation, shall carry the following documents in conformity with the conditions prescribed in this Convention:

(a) Its certificate of registration;

(b) Its certificate of airworthiness;

(c) The appropriate licences for each member of the crew;

(d) Its journey log book;

(e) If it is equipped with radio apparatus, the aircraft radio station licence;

(f) If it carries passengers, a list of their names and places of embarkation and destination;

(g) If it carries cargo, a manifest and detailed declarations of the cargo.

ARTICLE 30

Aircraft radio equipment

(a) Aircraft of each contracting State may, in or over the territory of other contracting States, carry radio transmitting apparatus only if a licence to install and operate such apparatus has been issued by the appropriate authorities of the State in which the aircraft is registered. The use of radio transmitting apparatus in the territory of the contracting State whose territory is flown over shall be in accordance with the regulations prescribed by that State.

(b) Radio transmitting apparatus may be used only by members of the flight crew who are provided with a special licence for the purpose, issued by the appropriate authorities of the State in which the aircraft is registered.

ARTICLE 31

Certificates of airworthiness

Every aircraft engaged in international navigation shall be provided with a certificate of airworthiness issued or rendered valid by the State in which it is registered.

ARTICLE 32

Licences of personnel

(a) The pilot of every aircraft and the other members of the operating crew of every aircraft engaged in international navigation shall be provided with certificates of competency and licences issued or rendered valid by the State in which the aircraft is registered.

(b) Each contracting State reserves the right to refuse to recognize, for the purpose of flight above its own territory, certificates of competency and licences granted to any of its nationals by another contracting State.

ARTICLE 33

Recognition of certificates and licences

Certificates of airworthiness and certificates of competency and licences issued or rendered valid by the contracting State in which the aircraft is registered, shall be recognized as valid by the other contracting States, provided that the requirements under which such certificates or licences were issued or rendered valid are equal to or above the minimum standards which may be established from time to time pursuant to this Convention.

ARTICLE 34

Journey log books

There shall be maintained in respect of every aircraft engaged in international navigation a journey log book in which shall be entered particulars of the aircraft, its crew and of each journey, in such form as may be prescribed from time to time pursuant to this Convention.

ARTICLE 35

Cargo restrictions

(a) No munitions of war or implements of war may be carried in or

97

above the territory of a State in aircraft engaged in international navigation, except by permission of such State. Each State shall determine by regulations what constitutes munitions of war or implements of war for the purposes of this Article, giving due consideration, for the purposes of uniformity, to such recommendations as the International Civil Aviation Organization may from time to time make.

(b) Each contracting State reserves the right, for reasons of public order and safety, to regulate or prohibit the carriage in or above its territory of articles other than those enumerated in paragraph (a): provided that no distinction is made in this respect between its national aircraft engaged in international navigation and the aircraft of the other States so engaged; and provided further that no restriction shall be imposed which may interfere with the carriage and use on aircraft of apparatus necessary for the operation or navigation of the aircraft or the safety of the personnel or passengers.

ARTICLE 36

Photographic apparatus

Each contracting State may prohibit or regulate the use of photographic apparatus in aircraft over its territory.

CHAPTER VI—INTERNATIONAL STANDARDS AND RECOMMENDED PRACTICES

ARTICLE 37

Adoption of international standards and procedures

Each contracting State undertakes to collaborate in securing the highest practicable degree of uniformity in regulations, standards, procedures, and organization in relation to aircraft, personnel, airways and auxiliary services in all matters in which such uniformity will facilitate and improve air navigation.

To this end the International Civil Aviation Organization shall adopt and amend from time to time, as may be necessary, international standards and recommended practices and procedures dealing with:

(a) Communications systems and air navigation aids, including ground marking;

(b) Characteristics of airports and landing areas;

(c) Rules of the air and air traffic control practices;

(d) Licensing of operating and mechanical personnel;

(e) Airworthiness of aircraft;

(f) Registration and identification of aircraft;

(g) Collection and exchange of meteorological information;

(h) Log books;

(i) Aeronautical maps and charts;

(j) Customs and immigration procedures;

(k) Aircraft in distress and investigation of accidents;

and such other matters concerned with the safety, regularity, and efficiency of air navigation as may from time to time appear appropriate.

ARTICLE 38

Departures from international standards and procedures

Any State which finds it impracticable to comply in all respects with any such international standard or procedure, or to bring its own regulations or practices into full accord with any international standard or procedure after amendment of the latter, or which deems it necessary to adopt regulations or practices differing in any particular respect from those established by an international standard, shall give immediate notification to the International Civil Aviation Organization of the differences between its own practice and that established by the international standard. In the case of amendments to international standards, any State which does not make the appropriate amendments to its own regulations or practices shall give notice to the Council within sixty days of the adoption of the amendment to the international standard, or indicate the action which it proposes to take. In any such case, the Council shall make immediate notification to all other States of the difference which exists between one or more features of an international standard and the corresponding national practice of that State.

ARTICLE 39

Endorsement of certificates and licences

(a) Any aircraft or part thereof with respect to which there exists an international standard of airworthiness or performance, and which failed in any respect to satisfy that standard at the time of its certification, shall have endorsed on or attached to its airworthiness certificate a complete enumeration of the details in respect of which it so failed.

(b) Any person holding a licence who does not satisfy in full the conditions laid down in the international standard relating to the class of licence or certificate which he holds shall have endorsed on or attached to his licence a complete enumeration of the particulars in which he does not satisfy such conditions.

ARTICLE 40

Validity of endorsed certificates and licences

No aircraft or personnel having certificates or licences so endorsed shall participate in international navigation, except with the permission of the State or States whose territory is entered. The registration or use of any such aircraft, or of any certificated aircraft part, in any State other than that in which it was originally certificated shall be at the discretion of the State into which the aircraft or part is imported.

ARTICLE 41

Recognition of existing standards of airworthiness

The provisions of this Chapter shall not apply to aircraft and aircraft equipment of types of which the prototype is submitted to the appropriate national authorities for certification prior to a date three years after the date of adoption of an international standard of airworthiness for such equipment.

ARTICLE 42

Recognition of existing standards of competency of personnel

The provisions of this Chapter shall not apply to personnel whose licences are originally issued prior to a date one year after initial adoption of an international standard of qualification for such personnel; but they shall in any case apply to all personnel whose licences remain valid five years after the date of adoption of such standard.

PART II

THE INTERNATIONAL CIVIL AVIATION ORGANIZATION

CHAPTER VII—THE ORGANIZATION

ARTICLE 43

Name and composition

An organization to be named the International Civil Aviation Organization is formed by the Convention. It is made up of an Assembly, a Council, and such other bodies as may be necessary.

ARTICLE 44

Objectives

The aims and objectives of the Organization are to develop the principles and techniques of international air navigation and to foster the planning and development of international air transport so as to:

(*a*) Insure the safe and orderly growth of international civil aviation throughout the world;

(*b*) Encourage the arts of aircraft design and operation for peaceful purposes;

(*c*) Encourage the development of airways, airports, and air navigation facilities for international civil aviation;

(*d*) Meet the needs of the peoples of the world for safe, regular, efficient and economical air transport;

(*e*) Prevent economic waste caused by unreasonable competition;

(*f*) Insure that the rights of contracting States are fully respected and that every contracting State has a fair opportunity to operate international airlines;

(g) Avoid discrimination between contracting States;

(h) Promote safety of flight in international air navigation;

(i) Promote generally the development of all aspects of international civil aeronautics.

ARTICLE 45[1]

Permanent seat

The permanent seat of the Organization shall be at such place as shall be determined at the final meeting of the Interim Assembly of the Provisional International Civil Aviation Organization set up by the Interim Agreement on International Civil Aviation signed at Chicago on 7 December 1944. The seat may be temporarily transferred elsewhere by decision of the Council, and otherwise than temporarily by decision of the Assembly, such decision to be taken by the number of votes specified by the Assembly. The number of votes so specified will not be less than three-fifths of the total number of contracting States.

ARTICLE 46

First meeting of Assembly

The first meeting of the Assembly shall be summoned by the Interim Council of the above-mentioned Provisional Organization as soon as the Convention has come into force, to meet at a time and place to be decided by the Interim Council.

ARTICLE 47

Legal capacity

The Organization shall enjoy in the territory of each contracting State such legal capacity as may be necessary for the performance of its functions. Full juridical personality shall be granted wherever compatible with the constitution and laws of the State concerned.

---

[1] This is the text of the Article as amended by the Eighth Session of the Assembly on 14 June 1954; it entered into force on 16 May 1958. Under Article 94 (a) of the Convention, the amended text is in force in respect of those States which have ratified the amendment. In respect of the States which have not ratified the amendment, the original Chicago text is still in force and, therefore, that text is reproduced below:

'The permanent seat of the Organization shall be at such place as shall be determined at the final meeting of the Interim Assembly of the Provisional International Civil Aviation Organization set up by the Interim Agreement on International Civil Aviation signed at Chicago on December 7, 1944. The seat may be temporarily transferred elsewhere by decision of the Council.'

As at 1 October 1964, this amendment had been ratified by 75 States.

101

CHAPTER VIII—THE ASSEMBLY

ARTICLE 48

Meetings of Assembly and voting

(a) The Assembly shall meet not less than once in three years and shall be convened by the Council at a suitable time and place. Extraordinary meetings of the Assembly may be held at any time upon the call of the Council or at the request of any ten contracting States addressed to the Secretary General.[1]

(b) All contracting States shall have an equal right to be represented at the meetings of the Assembly and each contracting State shall be entitled to one vote. Delegates representing contracting States may be assisted by technical advisers who may participate in the meetings but shall have no vote.

(c) A majority of the contracting States is required to constitute a quorum for the meetings of the Assembly. Unless otherwise provided in this Convention, decisions of the Assembly shall be taken by a majority of the votes cast.

ARTICLE 49

Powers and duties of Assembly

The powers and duties of the Assembly shall be to:

(a) Elect at each meeting its President and other officers;

(b) Elect the contracting States to be represented on the Council, in accordance with the provisions of Chapter IX;

(c) Examine and take appropriate action on the reports of the Council and decide on any matter referred to it by the Council;

(d) Determine its own rules of procedure and establish such subsidiary commissions as it may consider to be necessary or desirable;

---

[1] This is the text of the Article as amended by the Eighth Session of the Assembly on 14 June 1954; it entered into force on 12 December 1956. Under Article 94 (a) of the Convention, the amended text is in force in respect of those States which have ratified the amendment. In respect of the States which have not ratified the amendment, the original Chicago text is still in force and, therefore, that text is reproduced below:

'(a) The Assembly shall meet annually and shall be convened by the Council at a suitable time and place. Extraordinary meetings of the Assembly may be held at any time upon the call of the Council or at the request of any ten contracting States addressed to the Secretary General.'

As at 1 October 1964, this amendment had been ratified by 79 States. On 15 September 1962, there was signed in Rome a Protocol which proposed a further amendment of Article 48 (a). This would delete the second sentence and substitute for it the following text: 'An extraordinary meeting of the Assembly may be held at any time upon the call of the Council or at the request of not less than one-fifth of the total number of contracting States addressed to the Secretary General.' The proposed amendment was to come into force upon being ratified by 66 contracting States. As at 1 October 1964, only 33 ratifications had been obtained, and so the amendment was not yet in force.

(e) Vote annual budgets and determine the financial arrangements of the Organization, in accordance with the provisions of Chapter XII;[1]

(f) Review expenditures and approve the accounts of the Organization;

(g) Refer, at its discretion, to the Council, to subsidiary commissions, or to any other body any matter within its sphere of action;

(h) Delegate to the Council the powers and authority necessary or desirable for the discharge of the duties of the Organization and revoke or modify the delegations of authority at any time;

(i) Carry out the appropriate provisions of Chapter XIII;

(j) Consider proposals for the modification or amendment of the provisions of this Convention and, if it approves of the proposals, recommend them to the contracting States in accordance with the provisions of Chapter XXI;

(k) Deal with any matter within the sphere of action of the Organization not specifically assigned to the Council.

CHAPTER IX—THE COUNCIL

ARTICLE 50

Composition and election of Council

(a) The Council shall be a permanent body responsible to the Assembly. It shall be composed of twenty-seven contracting States elected by the Assembly. An election shall be held at the first meeting of the Assembly and thereafter every three years, and the members of the Council so elected shall hold office until the next following election.[2]

---

[1] This is the text of the Article as amended by the Eighth Session of the Assembly on 14 June 1954; it entered into force on 12 December 1956. Under Article 94 (a) of the Convention, the amended text is in force in respect of those States which have ratified the amendment. In respect of the States which have not ratified the amendment, the original Chicago text is still in force and, therefore, that text is reproduced below:

'(e) Vote an annual budget and determine the financial arrangements of the Organization, in accordance with the provisions of Chapter XII;'.

As at 1 October 1964, this amendment had been ratified by 79 States.

[2] This is the text of the Article as amended by the Thirteenth (Extraordinary) Session of the Assembly on 19 June 1961; it entered into force on 17 July 1962. Under Article 94 (a) of the Convention, the amended text is in force in respect of those States which have ratified the amendment. In respect of the States which have not ratified the amendment, the original Chicago text is still in force and, therefore, that text is reproduced below:

'(a) The Council shall be a permanent body responsible to the Assembly. It shall be composed of twenty-one contracting States elected by the Assembly. An election shall be held at the first meeting of the Assembly and thereafter every three years, and the members of the Council so elected shall hold office until the next following election.'

As at 1 October 1964, this amendment had been ratified by 76 States.

(b) In electing the members of the Council, the Assembly shall give adequate representation to (1) the States of chief importance in air transport; (2) the States not otherwise included which make the largest contribution to the provision of facilities for international civil air navigation; and (3) the States not otherwise included whose designation will insure that all the major geographic areas of the world are represented on the Council. Any vacancy on the Council shall be filled by the Assembly as soon as possible; any contracting State so elected to the Council shall hold office for the unexpired portion of its predecessor's term of office.

(c) No representative of a contracting State on the Council shall be actively associated with the operation of an international air service or financially interested in such a service.

ARTICLE 51

President of Council

The Council shall elect its President for a term of three years. He may be re-elected. He shall have no vote. The Council shall elect from among its members one or more Vice Presidents who shall retain their right to vote when serving as acting President. The President need not be selected from among the representatives of the members of the Council but, if a representative is elected, his seat shall be deemed vacant and it shall be filled by the State which he represented. The duties of the President shall be to:

(a) Convene meetings of the Council, the Air Transport Committee, and the Air Navigation Commission;

(b) Serve as representative of the Council; and

(c) Carry out on behalf of the Council the functions which the Council assigns to him.

ARTICLE 52

Voting in Council

Decisions by the Council shall require approval by a majority of its members. The Council may delegate authority with respect to any particular matter to a committee of its members. Decisions of any committee of the Council may be appealed to the Council by any interested contracting State.

ARTICLE 53

Participation without a vote

Any contracting State may participate, without a vote, in the consideration by the Council and by its committees and commissions of any question which especially affects its interests. No member of the Council shall vote in the consideration by the Council of a dispute to which it is a party.

ARTICLE 54

Mandatory functions of Council

The Council shall:

(a) Submit annual reports to the Assembly;

(b) Carry out the directions of the Assembly and discharge the duties and obligations which are laid on it by this Convention;

(c) Determine its organization and rules of procedure;

(d) Appoint and define the duties of an Air Transport Committee, which shall be chosen from among the representatives of the members of the Council, and which shall be responsible to it;

(e) Establish an Air Navigation Commission, in accordance with the provisions of Chapter X;

(f) Administer the finances of the Organization in accordance with the provisions of Chapters XII and XV;

(g) Determine the emoluments of the President of the Council;

(h) Appoint a chief executive officer who shall be called the Secretary General, and make provision for the appointment of such other personnel as may be necessary, in accordance with the provisions of Chapter XI;

(i) Request, collect, examine and publish information relating to the advancement of air navigation and the operation of international air services, including information about the costs of operation and particulars of subsidies paid to airlines from public funds;

(j) Report to contracting States any infraction of this Convention, as well as any failure to carry out recommendations or determinations of the Council;

(k) Report to the Assembly any infraction of this Convention where a contracting State has failed to take appropriate action within a reasonable time after notice of the infraction;

(l) Adopt, in accordance with the provisions of Chapter VI of this Convention, international standards and recommended practices; for convenience, designate them as Annexes to this Convention; and notify all contracting States of the action taken;

(m) Consider recommendations of the Air Navigation Commission for amendment of the Annexes and take action in accordance with the provisions of Chapter XX;

(n) Consider any matter relating to the Convention which any contracting State refers to it.

ARTICLE 55

Permissive functions of Council

The Council may:

(a) Where appropriate and as experience may show to be desirable, create subordinate air transport commissions on a regional or other basis and define groups of states or airlines with or through which it may deal to facilitate the carrying out of the aims of this Convention;

(b) Delegate to the Air Navigation Commission duties additional to those set forth in the Convention and revoke or modify such delegations of authority at any time;

(c) Conduct research into all aspects of air transport and air navigation which are of international importance, communicate the results of its research to the contracting States, and facilitate the exchange of information between contracting States on air transport and air navigation matters;

(d) Study any matters affecting the organization and operation of international air transport, including the international ownership and operation of international air services on trunk routes, and submit to the Assembly plans in relation thereto;

(e) Investigate, at the request of any contracting State, any situation which may appear to present avoidable obstacles to the development of international air navigation; and, after such investigation, issue such reports as may appear to it desirable.

CHAPTER X—THE AIR NAVIGATION COMMISSION

ARTICLE 56

Nomination and appointment of Commission

The Air Navigation Commission shall be composed of twelve members appointed by the Council from among persons nominated by contracting States. These persons shall have suitable qualifications and experience in the science and practice of aeronautics. The Council shall request all contracting States to submit nominations. The President of the Air Navigation Commission shall be appointed by the Council.

ARTICLE 57

Duties of Commission

The Air Navigation Commission shall:

(a) Consider, and recommend to the Council for adoption, modifications of the Annexes to this Convention;

(b) Establish technical subcommissions on which any contracting State may be represented, if it so desires;

(c) Advise the Council concerning the collection and communication to the contracting States of all information which it considers necessary and useful for the advancement of air navigation.

CHAPTER XI—PERSONNEL

ARTICLE 58

Appointment of personnel

Subject to any rules laid down by the Assembly and to the provisions of this Convention, the Council shall determine the method of appointment

106

and of termination of appointment, the training, and the salaries, allowances, and conditions of service of the Secretary General and other personnel of the Organization, and may employ or make use of the services of nationals of any contracting State.

ARTICLE 59

International character of personnel

The President of the Council, the Secretary General, and other personnel shall not seek or receive instructions in regard to the discharge of their responsibilities from any authority external to the Organization. Each contracting State undertakes fully to respect the international character of the responsibilities of the personnel and not to seek to influence any of its nationals in the discharge of their responsibilities.

ARTICLE 60

Immunities and privileges of personnel

Each contracting State undertakes, so far as possible under its constitutional procedure, to accord to the President of the Council, the Secretary General, and the other personnel of the Organization, the immunities and privileges which are accorded to corresponding personnel of other public international organizations. If a general international agreement on the immunities and privileges of international civil servants is arrived at, the immunities and privileges accorded to the President, the Secretary General, and the other personnel of the Organization shall be the immunities and privileges accorded under that general international agreement.

CHAPTER XII—FINANCE

ARTICLE 61[1]

Budget and apportionment of expenses

The Council shall submit to the Assembly annual budgets, annual

---

[1] This is the text of the Article as amended by the Eighth Session of the Assembly on 14 June 1954; it entered into force on 12 December 1956. Under Article 94 (*a*) of the Convention, the amended text is in force in respect of those States which have ratified the amendment. In respect of the States which have not ratified the amendment, the original Chicago text is still in force and, therefore, that text is reproduced below:

'The Council shall submit to the Assembly an annual budget, annual statements of accounts and estimates of all receipts and expenditures. The Assembly shall vote the budget with whatever modification it sees fit to prescribe and, with the exception of assessments under Chapter XV to States consenting thereto, shall apportion the expenses of the Organization among the contracting States on the basis which it shall from time to time determine.'

As at 1 October 1964, this amendment had been ratified by 79 States.

statements of accounts and estimates of all receipts and expenditures. The Assembly shall vote the budgets with whatever modification it sees fit to prescribe, and, with the exception of assessments under Chapter XV to States consenting thereto, shall apportion the expenses of the Organization among the contracting States on the basis which it shall from time to time determine.

ARTICLE 62

Suspension of voting power

The Assembly may suspend the voting power in the Assembly and in the Council of any contracting State that fails to discharge within a reasonable period its financial obligations to the Organization.

ARTICLE 63

Expenses of delegations and other representatives

Each contracting State shall bear the expenses of its own delegation to the Assembly and the remuneration, travel, and other expenses of any person whom it appoints to serve on the Council, and of its nominees or representatives on any subsidiary committees or commissions of the Organization.

CHAPTER XIII—OTHER INTERNATIONAL ARRANGEMENTS

ARTICLE 64

Security arrangements

The Organization may, with respect to air matters within its competence directly affecting world security, by vote of the Assembly enter into appropriate arrangements with any general organization set up by the nations of the world to preserve peace.

ARTICLE 65

Arrangements with other international bodies

The Council, on behalf of the Organization, may enter into agreements with other international bodies for the maintenance of common services and for common arrangements concerning personnel and, with the approval of the Assembly, may enter into such other arrangements as may facilitate the work of the Organization.

ARTICLE 66

Functions relating to other agreements

(*a*) The Organization shall also carry out the functions placed upon it by the International Air Services Transit Agreement and by the International Air Transport Agreement drawn up at Chicago on 7 December, 1944, in accordance with the terms and conditions therein set forth.

(b) Members of the Assembly and the Council who have not accepted the International Air Services Transit Agreement or the International Air Transport Agreement drawn up at Chicago on 7 December, 1944, shall not have the right to vote on any questions referred to the Assembly or Council under the provisions of the relevant Agreement.

PART III

INTERNATIONAL AIR TRANSPORT

CHAPTER XIV—INFORMATION AND REPORTS

ARTICLE 67

File reports with Council

Each contracting State undertakes that its international airlines shall. in accordance with requirements laid down by the Council, file with the Council traffic reports, cost statistics and financial statements showing among other things all receipts and the sources thereof.

CHAPTER XV—AIRPORTS AND OTHER AIR NAVIGATION FACILITIES

ARTICLE 68

Designation of routes and airports

Each contracting State may, subject to the provisions of this Convention, designate the route to be followed within its territory by any international air service and the airports which any such service may use.

ARTICLE 69

Improvement of air navigation facilities

If the Council is of the opinion that the airports or other air navigation facilities, including radio and meteorological services, of a contracting State are not reasonably adequate for the safe, regular, efficient, and economical operation of international air services, present or contemplated, the Council shall consult with the State directly concerned, and other States affected, with a view to finding means by which the situation may be remedied, and may make recommendations for that purpose. No contracting State shall be guilty of an infraction of this Convention if it fails to carry out these recommendations.

ARTICLE 70

Financing of air navigation facilities

A contracting State, in the circumstances arising under the provisions of Article 69, may conclude an arrangement with the Council for giving effect to such recommendations. The State may elect to bear all the costs involved in any such arrangement. If the State does not so elect, the Council may agree, at the request of the State, to provide for all or a portion of the costs.

ARTICLE 71

Provision and maintenance of facilities by Council

If a contracting State so requests, the Council may agree to provide, man, maintain, and administer any or all of the airports and other air navigation facilities including radio and meteorological services, required in its territory for the safe, regular, efficient and economical operation of the international air services of the other contracting States, and may specify just and reasonable charges for the use of facilities provided.

ARTICLE 72

Acquisition or use of land

Where land is needed for facilities financed in whole or in part by the Council at the request of a contracting State, that State shall either provide the land itself, retaining title if it wishes, or facilitate the use of the land by the Council on just and reasonable terms and in accordance with the laws of the State concerned.

ARTICLE 73

Expenditure and assessment of funds

Within the limit of the funds which may be made available to it by the Assembly under Chapter XII, the Council may make current expenditures for the purposes of this Chapter from the general funds of the Organization. The Council shall assess the capital funds required for the purposes of this Chapter in previously agreed proportions over a reasonable period of time to the contracting States consenting thereto whose airlines use the facilities. The Council may also assess to States that consent any working funds that are required.

ARTICLE 74

Technical assistance and utilization of revenues

When the Council, at the request of a contracting State, advances funds or provides airports or other facilities in whole or in part, the arrangement

110

may provide, with the consent of that State, for technical assistance in the supervision and operation of the airports and other facilities, and for the payment, from the revenues derived from the operation of the airports and other facilities, of the operating expenses of the airports and the other facilities, and of interest and amortization charges.

ARTICLE 75

Taking over of facilities from Council

A contracting State may at any time discharge any obligation into which it has entered under Article 70, and take over airports and other facilities which the Council has provided in its territory pursuant to the provisions of Articles 71 and 72, by paying to the Council an amount which in the opinion of the Council is reasonable in the circumstances. If the State considers that the amount fixed by the Council is unreasonable it may appeal to the Assembly against the decision of the Council and the Assembly may confirm or amend the decision of the Council.

ARTICLE 76

Return of funds

Funds obtained by the Council through reimbursement under Article 75 and from receipts of interest and amortization payments under Article 74 shall, in the case of advances originally financed by States under Article 73, be returned to the States which were originally assessed in the proportion of their assessments, as determined by the Council.

CHAPTER XVI—JOINT OPERATING ORGANIZATIONS AND POOLED SERVICES

ARTICLE 77

Joint operating organizations permitted

Nothing in this Convention shall prevent two or more contracting States from constituting joint air transport operating organizations or international operating agencies and from pooling their air services on any routes or in any regions, but such organizations or agencies and such pooled services shall be subject to all the provisions of this Convention, including those relating to the registration of agreements with the Council. The Council shall determine in what manner the provisions of this Convention relating to nationality of aircraft shall apply to aircraft operated by international operating agencies.

ARTICLE 78

Function of Council

The Council may suggest to contracting States concerned that they

111

form joint organizations to operate air services on any routes or in any regions.

ARTICLE 79

Participation in operating organizations

A State may participate in joint operating organizations or in pooling arrangements, either through its government or through an airline company or companies designated by its government. The companies may, at the sole discretion of the State concerned, be state-owned or partly state-owned or privately owned.

PART IV

FINAL PROVISIONS

CHAPTER XVII—OTHER AERONAUTICAL AGREEMENTS AND ARRANGEMENTS

ARTICLE 80

Paris and Habana Conventions

Each contracting State undertakes, immediately upon the coming into force of this Convention, to give notice of denunciation of the Convention relating to the Regulation of Aerial Navigation signed at Paris on 13 October 1919 or the Convention on Commercial Aviation signed at Habana on 20 February 1928, if it is a party to either. As between contracting States, this Convention supersedes the Conventions of Paris and Habana previously referred to.

ARTICLE 81

Registration of existing agreements

All aeronautical agreements which are in existence on the coming into force of this Convention, and which are between a contracting State and any other State or between an airline of a contracting State and any other State or the airline of any other State, shall be forthwith registered with the Council.

ARTICLE 82

Abrogation of inconsistent arrangements

The contracting States accept this Convention as abrogating all obligations and understandings between them which are inconsistent with its terms, and undertake not to enter into any such obligations and understandings. A contracting State which, before becoming a member of the Organization has undertaken any obligations toward a non-contracting

State or a national of a contracting State or of a non-contracting State inconsistent with the terms of this Convention, shall take immediate steps to procure its release from the obligations. If an airline of any contracting State has entered into any such inconsistent obligations, the State of which it is a national shall use its best efforts to secure their termination forthwith and shall in any event cause them to be terminated as soon as such action can lawfully be taken after the coming into force of this Convention.

ARTICLE 83

Registration of new arrangements

Subject to the provisions of the preceding Article, any contracting State may make arrangements not inconsistent with the provisions of this Convention. Any such arrangement shall be forthwith registered with the Council, which shall make it public as soon as possible.

CHAPTER XVIII—DISPUTES AND DEFAULT

ARTICLE 84

Settlement of disputes

If any disagreement between two or more contracting States relating to the interpretation or application of this Convention and its Annexes cannot be settled by negotiation, it shall, on the application of any State concerned in the disagreement, be decided by the Council. No member of the Council shall vote in the consideration by the Council of any dispute to which it is a party. Any contracting State may, subject to Article 85, appeal from the decision of the Council to an *ad hoc* arbitral tribunal agreed upon with the other parties to the dispute or to the Permanent Court of International Justice. Any such appeal shall be notified to the Council within sixty days of receipt of notification of the decision of the Council.

ARTICLE 85

Arbitration procedure

If any contracting State party to a dispute in which the decision of the Council is under appeal has not accepted the Statute of the Permanent Court of International Justice and the contracting States parties to the dispute cannot agree on the choice of the arbitral tribunal, each of the contracting States parties to the dispute shall name a single arbitrator who shall name an umpire. If either contracting State party to the dispute fails to name an arbitrator within a period of three months from the date of the appeal, an arbitrator shall be named on behalf of that State by the President of the Council from a list of qualified and available persons maintained by the Council. If, within thirty days, the arbitrators cannot agree on an umpire, the President of the Council shall designate an umpire from the list previously referred to. The arbitrators and the umpire shall then jointly constitute an arbitral tribunal. Any arbitral tribunal established under this or the preceding Article shall settle its own procedure and give its decisions by majority vote, provided that the Council may determine procedural questions in the event of any delay which in the opinion of the Council is excessive.

ARTICLE 86

Appeals

Unless the Council decides otherwise any decision by the Council on whether an international airline is operating in conformity with the provisions of this Convention shall remain in effect unless reversed on appeal. On any other matter, decisions of the Council shall, if appealed from, be suspended until the appeal is decided. The decisions of the Permanent Court of International Justice and of an arbitral tribunal shall be final and binding.

ARTICLE 87

Penalty for non-conformity of airline

Each contracting State undertakes not to allow the operation of an airline of a contracting State through the air space above its territory if the Council has decided that the airline concerned is not conforming to a final decision rendered in accordance with the previous Article.

ARTICLE 88

Penalty for non-conformity by State

The Assembly shall suspend the voting power in the Assembly and in the Council of any contracting State that is found in default under the provisions of this Chapter.

CHAPTER XIX—WAR

ARTICLE 89

War and emergency conditions

In case of war, the provisions of this Convention shall not affect the freedom of action of any of the contracting States affected, whether as belligerents or as neutrals. The same principle shall apply in the case of any contracting State which declares a state of national emergency and notifies the fact to the Council.

Chapter XX—Annexes

Article 90

Adoption and amendment of Annexes

(a) The adoption by the Council of the Annexes described in Article 54, subparagraph (*l*), shall require the vote of two-thirds of the Council at a meeting called for that purpose and shall then be submitted by the Council to each contracting State. Any such Annex or any amendment of an Annex shall become effective within three months after its submission to the contracting States or at the end of such longer period of time as the Council may prescribe, unless in the meantime a majority of the contracting States register their disapproval with the Council.

(b) The Council shall immediately notify all contracting States of the coming into force of any Annex or amendment thereto.

Chapter XXI—Ratifications, Adherences, Amendments, and Denunciations

Article 91

Ratification of Convention

(a) This Convention shall be subject to ratification by the signatory States. The instruments of ratification shall be deposited in the archives of the Government of the United States of America, which shall give notice of the date of the deposit to each of the signatory and adhering States.

(b) As soon as this Convention has been ratified or adhered to by twenty-six States it shall come into force between them on the thirtieth day after deposit of the twenty-sixth instrument. It shall come into force for each State ratifying thereafter on the thirtieth day after the deposit of its instrument of ratification.

(ι) It shall be the duty of the Government of the United States of America to notify the government of each of the signatory and adhering States of the date on which this Convention comes into force.

Article 92

Adherence to Convention

(a) This Convention shall be open for adherence by members of the United Nations and States associated with them, and States which remained neutral during the present world conflict.

(b) Adherence shall be effected by a notification addressed to the Government of the United States of America and shall take effect as from the thirtieth day from the receipt of the notification by the Government of the United States of America, which shall notify all the contracting States.

115

ARTICLE 93

Admission of other States

States other than those provided for in Articles 91 and 92 (*a*) may, subject to approval by any general international organization set up by the nations of the world to preserve peace, be admitted to participation in this Convention by means of a four-fifths vote of the Assembly and on such conditions as the Assembly may prescribe: provided that in each case the assent of any State invaded or attacked during the present war by the State seeking admission shall be necessary.

ARTICLE 93 BIS[1]

(*a*) Notwithstanding the provisions of Articles 91, 92 and 93 above:

(*1*) A State whose government the General Assembly of the United Nations has recommended be debarred from membership in international agencies established by or brought into relationship with the United Nations shall automatically cease to be a member of the International Civil Aviation Organization;

(*2*) A State which has been expelled from membership in the United Nations shall automatically cease to be a member of the International Civil Aviation Organization unless the General Assembly of the United Nations attaches to its act of expulsion a recommendation to the contrary.

(*b*) A State which ceases to be a member of the International Civil Aviation Organization as a result of the provisions of paragraph (*a*) above may, after approval by the General Assembly of the United Nations, be readmitted to the Internation Civil Aviation Organization upon application and upon approval by a majority of the Council.

(*c*) Members of the Organization which are suspended from the exercise of the rights and privileges of membership in the United Nations shall, upon the request of the latter, be suspended from the rights and privileges of membership in this Organization.

ARTICLE 94

Amendment of Convention

(*a*) Any proposed amendment to this Convention must be approved by a two-thirds vote of the Assembly and shall then come into force in respect of States which have ratified such amendment when ratified by the number of contracting States specified by the Assembly. The number so specified shall not be less than two-thirds of the total number of contracting States.

(*b*) If in its opinion the amendment is of such a nature as to justify this course, the Assembly in its resolution recommending adoption may provide that any State which has not ratified within a specified period after

---

[1] On 27 May 1947 the Assembly decided to amend the Chicago Convention by introducing Article 93 bis. Under Article 94 (*a*) of the Convention the amendment came into force on 20 March 1961 in respect of States which ratified it. As at 1 October 1964, this amendment had been ratified by 48 States.

the amendment has come into force shall thereupon cease to be a member of the Organization and a party to the Convention.

ARTICLE 95
Denunciation of Convention

(a) Any contracting State may give notice of denunciation of this Convention three years after its coming into effect by notification addressed to the Government of the United States of America, which shall at once inform each of the contracting States.

(b) Denunciation shall take effect one year from the date of the receipt of the notification and shall operate only as regards the State effecting the denunciation.

CHAPTER XXII—DEFINITIONS

ARTICLE 96

For the purpose of this Convention the expression:

(a) 'Air service' means any scheduled air service performed by aircraft for the public transport of passengers, mail or cargo.

(b) 'International air service' means an air service which passes through the air space over the territory of more than one State.

(c) 'Airline' means any air transport enterprise offering or operating an international air service.

(d) 'Stop for non-traffic purposes' means a landing for any purpose other than taking on or discharging passengers, cargo or mail.

SIGNATURE OF CONVENTION

IN WITNESS WHEREOF, the under-signed plenipotentiaries, having been duly authorized, sign this Convention on behalf of their respective governments on the dates appearing opposite their signatures.

DONE at Chicago the seventh day of December 1944, in the English language. A text drawn up in the English, French and Spanish languages,[1]

---

[1] The Convention was signed in the English original version formulated at the International Civil Aviation Conference which took place at Chicago from 1 November to 7 December 1944. No trilingual text has been opened for signature as provided for in the Convention.
The Government of the United States of America in the note of the State Department of 22 September 1947 addressed to the Chiefs of Mission of the Governments concerned, after having drawn their attention to the various problems involved in this respect and to the fact that the Convention as drawn up at the Chicago Conference did not place a specific responsibility upon the United States Government, as depository of the Convention, to prepare the trilingual text, concluded: 'The Department of State considers that it is not advisable to proceed at this time with preparations to open for signature at Washington

each of which shall be of equal authenticity, shall be open for signature at Washington, D.C. Both texts shall be deposited in the archives of the Government of the United States of America, and certified copies shall be transmitted by that Government to the governments of all the States which may sign or adhere to this Convention.

The Assembly of the International Civil Aviation Organization, at its Third Session (1949), resolved:

A3-2: *Preparation of French and Spanish texts of the Convention*

BE IT RESOLVED:
That the Council take action with a view to providing the Organization as soon as possible with texts of the Chicago Convention on International Civil Aviation in Spanish and French, it being understood that these texts will be used only for the internal purposes of the Organization.

At the Ninth Meeting of its Fifteenth Session on 19 February 1952, the Council of the Organization adopted the following Resolution:

THE COUNCIL,
CONSIDERING Resolution A3-2 which relates to the preparation of texts of the Chicago Convention in French and Spanish and specified that it should be 'understood that these texts will be used only for the internal purposes of the Organization'.

RESOLVES that the texts in French and Spanish attached to this Resolution shall be used, in addition to the English text signed at Chicago, for the internal purposes of the Organization, *i.e.* for work of the Secretariat, the Assembly, the Council and other bodies of the Organization and for any reference to be made by the Organization in communications to Contracting States.

RECOMMENDS to Contracting States that, for reference purposes in their relations with ICAO or with other Contracting States, they use these three texts only, and

DIRECTS the Secretary General to make arrangements for the publication of the English, French and Spanish texts in a single document.

---

trilingual texts of those documents. On the contrary, the United States Government proposes to present the question to the Council of the International Civil Aviation Organization with a request that the question be placed on the agenda for the next meeting of the Assembly of that Organization. It is believed that this procedure will afford the most efficacious means by which the governments concerned may, after due consideration of all the factors and problems involved, make such decisions with respect thereto as they deem appropriate.'

(B) LIST OF PARTIES

As at 1 October 1964, the following States, having duly ratified it or adhered to it, were Parties to the Convention on International Civil Aviation signed at Chicago on 7 December 1944.

Afghanistan
Algeria
Argentina
Australia
Austria

Belgium
Bolivia
Brazil
Burma

Cambodia
Cameroun
Central African Republic
Ceylon
Chad
Chile
China
Colombia
Congo (Brazzaville)
Congo (Leopoldville)
Costa Rica
Cuba
Cyprus
Czechoslovakia

Dahomey
Denmark
Dominican Republic

Ecuador
El Salvador
Ethiopia

Finland
France

Gabon
Germany (Federal Republic of)
Ghana
Greece
Guatemala
Guinea

Haiti
Honduras

Iceland
India
Indonesia
Iran
Iraq
Ireland
Israel
Italy
Ivory Coast

Jamaica
Japan
Jordan

Kenya
Korea (Republic of)
Kuwait

Laos
Lebanon
Liberia
Libya
Luxembourg

Malagasy Republic
Malawi
Malaysia (Federation of)
Mali
Mauritania
Mexico
Morocco

Nepal
Netherlands
New Zealand
Nicaragua
Niger
Nigeria
Norway

119

Pakistan
Panama
Paraguay
Peru
Philippines
Poland
Portugal

Rwanda

Saudi Arabia
Senegal
Sierra Leone
Somalia
South Africa (Republic of)
Spain
Sudan
Sweden
Switzerland
Syrian Arab Republic

Tanganyika and Zanzibar (United Republic of)[1]
Thailand
Trinidad and Tobago
Tunisia
Turkey

United Arab Republic
United Kingdom
United States
Upper Volta
Uruguay

Venezuela
Viet Nam

Yemen
Yugoslavia

[1] On 26 October 1964 the name of this country was changed to 'United Republic of Tanzania'.

BIBLIOGRAPHY

FOR FURTHER REFERENCE

Abbreviations:

A.J.I.L. = *American Journal of International Law*
B.Y.I.L. = *British Year Book of International Law*
C.L.P. = *Current Legal Problems*
I.C.L.Q. = *International and Comparative Law Quarterly*
J.A.L.C. = *Journal of Air Law and Commerce*
R.C.A.D.I. = *Recueil des Cours de l'Académie de Droit International*
R.G.D.I.P. = *Revue Générale de Droit International Public*

A. GENERAL

BILLYOU, DE F. *Air Law* (1963). New York, Ad Press.

CHENG, BIN. *The Law of International Air Transport* (1962). London, Stevens.

COOPER, J. C. *The Right to Fly* (1947). New York, Holt.

Encyclopaedia Britannica, 15th edition. Sections on Aerial Law, Aerial Navigation, Aeronautics, Airship, Air Forces, Air Warfare, Aviation, Balloons.

GOEDHUIS, D. 'Questions of Public International Air Law', *R.C.A.D.I.*, 81 (1952) p. 205.

JENNINGS, R. Y. 'Some Aspects of the International Law of the Air', *R.C.A.D.I.*, 75 (1949) p. 509.

LE GOFF, M. *Manuel de droit aérien: droit public* (1954); *droit privé* (1961). Paris, Librairie Dalloz.

LEMOINE, M. *Traité de droit aérien* (1947). Paris, Librairie du Recueil Sirey.

LISSITZYN, O. 1 *International Air Transport and National Policy* (1942). New York, Council on Foreign Relations.

MATTE, N. M. *Traité de droit aérien-aeronautique* (2nd ed., 1964). Paris, Editions A. Pedone.

McNAIR, Lord. *The Law of the Air* (3rd ed., by M. R. E. Kerr and A. H. M. Evans, 1964). London, Stevens.

PÉPIN, E. 'Le droit aérien', *R.C.A.D.I.*, 71 (1947) p. 481.

SAND, P. H., FREITAS, J. de S. and PRATT, G. N. 'An Historical Survey of International Air Law before the Second World War', *McGill Law Journal*, 7 (1960-1) p. 24.

SAND, P. H., LYON, J. T. and PRATT, G. N. 'An Historical Survey of International Air Law since 1944', *McGill Law Journal*, 7 (1960-1) p. 125.

SHAWCROSS, C. N. and BEAUMONT, K. M. *Air Law* (2nd ed. 1951, and 2nd (cumulative) supplement, 1955). London, Butterworth.

B. SPECIAL

CHAPTERS I AND II

BALDWIN, S. E. 'The Law of the Air-Ship', *A.J.I.L.*, 4 (1910) p. 95.

COOPER, J. C. 'The International Air Navigation Conference in Paris, 1910', *J.A.L.C.*, 19 (1952) p. 127.

ELLIS, W. E. 'Aerial-land and Aerial-maritime Warfare', *A.J.I.L.*, 8 (1914) p. 256.

FAUCHILLE, P. 'Le domaine aérien et le régime juridique des aerostats', *R.G.D.I.P.*, 8 (1901) p. 414.

'La circulation aérienne et les droits des états en temps de paix', *R.G.D.I.P.* 17 (1910) p. 55.

HAZELTINE, H. D. *The Law of the Air* (1911). London, University of London Press.

HERSHEY, A. S. 'The International Law of Aerial Space', *A.J.I.L.*, 6 (1912) p. 381.[1]

HIGGINS, A. PEARCE. *The Hague Peace Conferences and Other International Conferences concerning the Laws and Usages of War* (1909). Cambridge University Press.

INSTITUT DE DROIT INTERNATIONAL. Annuaire 19 (1902) p. 19; Annuaire 21 (1906) p. 293; Annuaire 23 (1910) p. 297; Annuaire 24 (1911) p. 303.

INTERNATIONAL LAW ASSOCIATION. Report of 28th Conference, Madrid, 1913.

KUHN, A. K. 'The Beginnings of an Aerial Law', *A.J.I.L.*, 4 (1910) p. 109.

LEE, B. 'Sovereignty of the Air', *A.J.I.L.*, 7 (1913) p. 470.

RICHARDS, SIR H. ERLE. *Sovereignty over the Air*. (A lecture delivered before the University of Oxford on 26 October 1912, and published by the Clarendon Press.)

ROLLAND, L. 'L'accord franco-allemand du 26 juillet 1913 relatif à la navigation aérienne', *R.G.D.I.P.*, 20 (1913) p. 697.

SCOTT, J. B. (editor). *The Hague Conventions and Declarations of 1899 and 1907* (2nd ed.) New York, Carnegie Endowment for International Peace, 1915.

CHAPTER III

GARNER, J. W. *International Law and the World War*, 2 volumes (1920). London, Longmans, Green.

'Proposed Rules for the Regulation of Aerial Warfare', *A.J.I.L.*, 18 (1924) p. 56.

RICHARDS, SIR H. ERLE. *International Law: Some Problems of the War*. (A lecture delivered before the University of Oxford on 30 October 1915, and published by the Clarendon Press.)

RODGERS, W. L. 'The Laws of War concerning Aviation and Radio', *A.J.I.L.*, 17 (1923) p. 629.

[1] See also, at p. 485 of this number of the *A.J.I.L.*, an anonymous article entitled 'The Use of Balloons in the War between Italy and Turkey'.

BIBLIOGRAPHY

ROPER, A. *La convention internationale du 13 octobre 1919* (1930). Paris, Librairie du Recueil Sirey.
SLOTEMAKER, L. H. *Freedom of Passage for International Air Services* (1932). Leiden, A. W. Sijthoff.
SPAIGHT, J. M. *Air Power and War Rights* (2nd ed. 1933). London, Longmans, Green.
TOMBS, L. C. *International Organization in European Air Transport* (1936). New York, Columbia University Press.

CHAPTER IV

HARRIS, SIR ARTHUR. *Bomber Offensive* (1947). London, Collins.
IRVING, DAVID. *The Destruction of Dresden* (1963). London, William Kimber.
JENNINGS, R. Y. 'Open Towns', *B.Y.I.L.* 22 (1945), p. 258.
SCHWARZENBERGER, G. 'The Law of Air Warfare and the Trend Towards Total War', *University of Malaya Law Review*, 1 (1959), p. 120.
The Legality of Nuclear Weapons (1958). London, Stevens.
'Report on Self-Defence under the Charter of the United Nations and the Use of Prohibited Weapons', *International Law Association*, Report of the 50th Conference, Brussels, 1962.
SPAIGHT, J. M. *Air Power and War Rights* (3rd ed., 1947). London, Longmans, Green.
WEBSTER, SIR CHARLES and FRANKLAND, N. *The Strategic Air Offensive against Germany*, 4 volumes (1961). London, Her Majesty's Stationery Office.

CHAPTER V

CHENG, BIN. 'Recent Developments in Air Law', *C.L.P.*, 9 (1956) p. 208.
'Centrifugal Tendencies in Air Law', *C.L.P.*, 10 (1957) p. 200.
'International Law and High Altitude Flights: Balloons, Rockets and Man-made Satellites', *I.C.L.Q.*, 6 (1957) p. 487.
'State Ships and State Aircraft', *C.L.P.*, 11 (1958) p. 225.
'Crimes on Board Aircraft', *C.L.P.*, 12 (1959) p. 177.
'From Air Law to Space Law', *C.L.P.*, 13 (1960) p. 228.
'The United Nations and Outer Space', *C.L.P.*, 14 (1961) p. 247.
COOPER, J. C. 'National Status of Aircraft', *J.A.L.C.*, 17 (1950) p. 292.
HONIG, J. P. *The Legal Status of Aircraft* (1956). The Hague, Martinus Nijhoff.
INTERNATIONAL LAW ASSOCIATION. Reports on 'Crime in Aircraft' by Arnold W. Knauth and Alex Mayer. (Report of 48th Conference, New York, 1958.)
LISSITZYN, O. J. 'The Treatment of Aerial Intruders', *A.J.I.L.*, 47 (1953) p. 559.
'Some Legal Implications of the U2 and RB 47 Incidents', *A.J.I.L.*, 56 (1962) p. 135.
MCMAHON, J. F. 'Legal Aspects of Outer Space', *B.Y.I.L.*, 38 (1962) p. 339.
SCHENKMAN, J. *International Civil Aviation Organization* (1955). Geneva, Librairie E. Droz.

BIBLIOGRAPHY

THOMAS, A. J. *Economic Regulation of Scheduled Air Transport* (1951). Buffalo, N.Y., Dennis.

WHEATCROFT, S. *The Economics of European Air Transport* (1956). Manchester University Press.

Air Transport Policy (1964). London, Michael Joseph.

WILBERFORCE, Lord. 'Some Recent Developments in the International Law of Aviation', *Transactions of the Grotius Society for the Year 1949*, Vol. 35, p. 73.

WRIGHT, Q. 'Legal Aspects of the U2 Incident', *A.J.I.L.*, 54 (1960) p. 836.

INDEX

active nationality principle, 75
Aerial Navigation Acts: (1911), 22, 36; (1913), 22, 36
Aeronautical Commission (1919), 33
aerospace, 4
aérostats, 12 and n.
air carriers, liability, 37, 38
Air Corporations Act (1949), 70
Air Force (Constitution) Act (1917), 45
air law, autonomy of, 4
Air Navigation Acts: (1920), 36; (1947), 70
air raids:
    in World War I, 27 ff.
    in World War II, 47 ff.
air routes, exchange of, 66 f.
air space:
    limits of, 60
    status of, 32, 60
    see also sovereignty
Air Transport Advisory Council, 70
Air Transport Licensing Board, 70
airways, international, 35
airworthiness, certificates of, 24, 34
Alcock and Brown, 9
Alverstone, Lord, 28
American aircraft, alleged trespasses over air space of other countries, 71 f.
American Civil War, 8
Arlandes, Marquis d', 7
arming of aircraft, 26
Attlee, C. R. [Earl], 52
aviation, commercial, beginnings, 9

Baird, Major, 31
Baldwin, J.E.A., 49
Baldwin, Stanley [Earl], 44
Balfour, A. J. [Earl], 27 f.
balloons:
    first use of, 7
    military use of, 7 f., 11
    observation, shooting down, 27
    'trespassing' by, 70 f.
Basdevant, Prof., 39

Bell, Rt. Rev. G. K. (Bishop of Chichester), 50
Bermuda Agreement, 67, 69
Blackburn, Judge, 15
Blackstone, Sir Wm., 14
Blanchard, François, 7
Bleriot, Louis, 8
blockade, and air bombardment, comparison, 53
bombardment, aerial:
    area, 50, 52 f.
    for occupation and for destruction, 31, 32
    when legitimate, 42
    limitation of, 41 f.
    naval, 19 f.
    regulations and rules governing, 18 f., 54 f.
    suggested prohibition, 38
    terror, 51 f., 57
    of undefended places, 19, 27
    see also air raids
Bottomley, N. H., 48, 49
Bowett, D. W., 57n.
Brabner, Commander, 51
British Overseas Airways Act (1939), 70
Brownlie, I., 57n.
Bryce, Lord, 28
Buckmaster, Lord, 29
Bulgaria, alleged trespass by Israeli aircraft over, 72 f.
bullets:
    incendiary, 26, 40
    small explosive, 10 f., 40
    tracer, 26 f., 40

cabotage, 34
Canterbury, Convocation, 29
capacity:
    pre-determination of, 68
    principles regarding, 68
Carriage by Air Acts: (1932), 37; (1961) 37
Carriage by Air (Parties to Convention) Orders, 37

125